United States Presidents

Jimmy Carter

Anne Schraff

Enslow Publishers, Inc.

44 Fadem Road	PO Box 38
Box 699	Aldershot
Springfield, NJ 07081	Hants GU12 6BP
USA	UK

Library of Congress Cataloging-in-Publication Data

Schraff, Anne E.
    Jimmy Carter / Anne Schraff.
       p. cm. — (United States presidents)
    Summary: Traces the life of the thirty-ninth president from his
childhood in Plains, Georgia, through his career in the Navy, to his
term in the White House, as well as his later humanitarian and
diplomatic efforts.
    Includes bibliographical references and index.
    ISBN 0-89490-935-5
    1. Carter, Jimmy, 1924 –   —Juvenile literature. 2. Presidents—
United States—Biography—Juvenile literature. [1. Carter, Jimmy,
1924–   . 2. Presidents.] I. Title. II. Series.
E873.S36 1998
973. 926'092—dc21
    [B]   97-20275
                                                           CIP
                                                           AC

Printed in the United States of America

10 9 8 7 6 5 4 3

Illustration Credits: Jimmy Carter Library, pp. 10, 13, 15, 21,
23, 25, 43, 50, 54, 58, 64, 66, 68, 73, 85.

Source Document Credits: Jimmy Carter Library, pp. 34, 40,
47, 51, 53, 60, 70, 74, 78, 87, 90–91.

Cover Illustration: Jimmy Carter Library

Contents

1 Triumph at Camp David 5

2 From Plains to Annapolis 9

3 Marriage and the
United States Navy 18

4 Home to Plains and Politics 28

5 A Run for the White House 36

6 A Domestic Agenda 45

7 Human Rights and Panama 56

8 China, SALT, and
Storm Over Iran 63

9 The Hostage Crisis 76

10 After the Presidency 89

Chronology 98

Chapter Notes 100

Further Reading 108

Internet Addresses 109

Index 111

1

TRIUMPH AT CAMP DAVID

O n September 6, 1978, President Jimmy Carter felt like a soldier going into battle.[1] Carter was trying to bring peace to the Middle East. He brought Egypt's President Anwar Sadat and Israel's Prime Minister Menachem Begin to Camp David, Maryland. Camp David is a woodsy vacation spot where American Presidents go to relax. There are many small cottages and peaceful trails for walking. At that time, there was a war between Israel and Egypt. Carter wanted them to sign a peace treaty while at Camp David.

The State of Israel declared itself a nation on May 15, 1948. Jews had been living there for centuries. Arabs lived there, too. The Arabs did not want a Jewish state. So just a few hours after Israel became a nation, the armies of the six Arab states attacked Israel. During the next thirty years, Israel and the Arab nations fought four wars. They were bitter enemies. Egypt was one of these Arab nations.

President Carter first met Sadat in 1977. Carter asked Sadat if peace was possible between Egypt and Israel. "Not in my lifetime," Sadat snapped.[2] Carter did not give up. He kept on writing letters to Begin and Sadat. Carter liked both men, but he felt closer to Sadat.[3] Carter treated Sadat like a member of his own family.[4]

When the meetings at Camp David began, Carter let Begin and Sadat do most of the talking. Carter just made notes as they argued. Carter wanted to give them time to get to know one another. Then Carter joined in the talks. When the arguments got too heated, he smoothed things over.

On the tenth day of the meetings, everything seemed to be going well. Sadat and Begin agreed on many things. Carter hoped a peace treaty would be signed at Camp David. Then Sadat began to complain about Jewish people in Israel living on land that belonged to Arab people. Sadat said those Jewish people had to move and give the land back to Arab families. Begin refused to do this. "My right eye will fall out, my right hand will fall off before I ever agree to the dismantling of a single Jewish settlement," Begin said.[5]

President Carter had been so hopeful for success. Now he was afraid the meeting would end in bitterness. The people of the world hoped for peace in the Middle

East. It seemed that Carter would have to tell them that Camp David had failed.

Carter hoped that at least Begin and Sadat would part as friends, bringing hope for future meetings.[6] Then Carter heard terrible news from American Secretary of State Cyrus Vance, who had just spoken to Sadat. Vance rushed into Carter's cottage to say, "Sadat has packed his bags. His bags are packed. He has asked for a helicopter and he's leaving."[7] Carter was shocked and did not know what to do.[8] If Sadat left Camp David in anger, the chances for peace would be dim.

Carter looked out the window of his cottage. He did what he often did at such times—he prayed that a way could be found to save the Camp David meeting.[9]

Carter went to Sadat's cottage. It was just as Vance said. Sadat and his aides were standing on the porch. They were ready to go. Sadat looked pale and nervous. Carter walked up to Sadat and asked him to step inside. Carter knew that his every word was important now. Carter had never been so serious about anything in his life.[10]

Carter looked Sadat in the eye and said, "Have you really thought about what this means?" Sadat said that he had thought about it. Carter continued, "It will mean first of all an end to the relationship between the United States and Egypt. There is no way we can ever explain this to our people. It would mean an end to this peace-keeping effort." Then Carter spoke the most important words of all. ". . . it will mean the end of something that is very precious to me: my friendship with you. Why are you doing it?"[11] At those words, Sadat decided not to leave after all.

Carter then went to see Begin. He begged him to compromise on the issue of Jewish settlements. Begin became angry. He said Carter was demanding too much. He said he could not ask those Jewish settlers to move off the land so dear to them. Begin said that if he did this the Jewish voters of Israel would throw him out of office.[12] Carter kept on talking. He asked Begin to think it over just a little more. Finally, Begin gave in. He said he would ask the Israel Parliament, the Knesset, to vote on the issue. If the Knesset agreed, the Jewish settlers would move.

Begin and Sadat sat down together again. With Carter urging them on, they finally agreed. Sadat was willing to let the Knesset vote on the settlement issue.

On the thirteenth day of the meeting, September 17, 1978, a peace-treaty outline was written. Begin and Sadat signed it. It ended the state of war that had existed between Israel and Egypt for thirty years. This war had cost the lives of thousands of Egyptians and Israelis. Now there would be peace between these once bitter enemies.

For President Jimmy Carter, it was a wonderful moment. He had worked harder on this problem than on any other. "For a few hours, all three of us were flushed with pride and good will toward one another because of our unexpected success," Carter said.[13]

2

FROM PLAINS TO ANNAPOLIS

J ames Earl Carter, Jr., was born in the small farming town of Plains, Georgia, on October 1, 1924. Everybody called him Jimmy. Plains is about one hundred twenty miles south of Atlanta, Georgia. The most important crops grown in Plains were peanuts, cotton, corn, watermelon, and potatoes.

Jimmy's father was James Earl Carter, known as Earl. He came to Plains as a small boy in 1904. He had been a soldier in World War I (1914–1918) before he came home to farm in Plains. Earl Carter was a hard-working farmer who also ran a small store in town. He sold items like overalls, feed, seed, and farm tools. Earl Carter was interested in his town, so he served on the county school board. He worked with the Rural Electrification Association (REA) and helped bring

James Earl Carter, Jr., the oldest child of the family, was born in Plains, Georgia, on October 1, 1924.

electricity to Plains. He was a tough-minded, independent man who was respected in Plains.[1]

Jimmy's mother was born Lillian Gordy. She was one of eight children. Her father was postmaster. Lillian Gordy was strong minded and outspoken.[2] She was a nursing student when she met Earl Carter. They were married in 1923. Lillian Carter worked as a nurse in Plains Sanitarium, a hospital.

Outside Plains, there was a settlement named Archery. About one hundred African Americans lived there. They helped farm the Carter land and other nearby farms. At that time, black and white southerners lived in separate neighborhoods. The children went to separate schools. Earl Carter believed in segregation (the separation of the races). Most people of his time in the South did. So when African Americans came to the Carter home, Earl Carter let them in the back door. Whites used the front door.[3]

Lillian Carter did not believe in segregation, however. She was the first person in Plains to treat black and white people equally. When she was home, black visitors used the front door. They sat at the table with her family. Earl Carter did not say anything when this happened. He just walked away.[4]

Jimmy Carter later said, "I'm much more like my mother than I am my father. She read day and night, at the breakfast table, the lunch table, the supper table."[5] As her children were growing up, Lillian Carter often rushed off to a neighbor's house where there was illness. She took care of the sick, both black and white.

Jimmy Carter was the first child born to the family. Two years later, in 1926, Jimmy's sister, Gloria, was born. In 1929, his sister Ruth was born. The last child was Billy, born in 1937. The Carters lived in a wooden farmhouse shaded by many trees, which made it cool in summer. In winter, the only heat came from two fireplaces and the kitchen stove. On very cold winter nights, the Carters heated bricks on the stove. Then they wrapped the bricks in cloth and took them to bed to keep warm. When Jimmy was a boy, there was no electricity or indoor plumbing in the house. Plains had no movie theater or library.[6] When children wanted to have fun, they had to think of things to do on their own.

Jimmy and his friends had a homemade swimming pool on the farm. The pool was five feet wide, fifteen feet long, and five feet deep. It was lined on the sides with boards. On hot summer days, it was the place to be. Jimmy also had his own pony, named Lady, as well as horses and mules to ride.

Jimmy kept a pet alligator in a box under his bed. He spent many hours fishing for catfish and white suckers, a not-so-tasty freshwater fish. Jimmy often went dove hunting with his father at sunrise. He also made and flew kites and caught lightning bugs, then set them free. Sometimes, Jimmy and his friends put pennies on the railroad tracks for the train wheels to flatten. They gave the flat pennies away as gifts. While still small, Jimmy

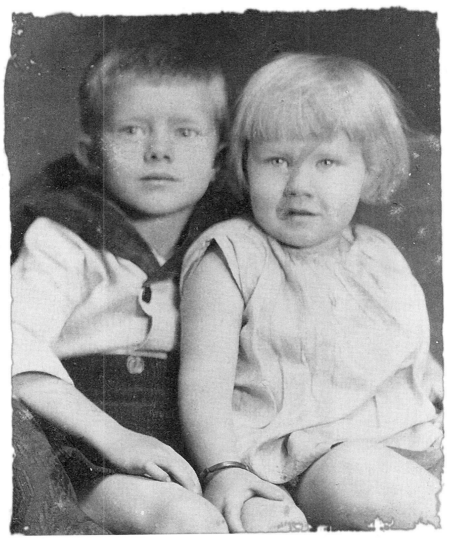

Carter with his younger sister Gloria. The Carter children did not have the comforts of electricity or indoor plumbing.

hunted, fished, and built tree houses with the African-American boys from Archery.

Life was not only play, however. There were many chores. Jimmy's father was very strict with him. When Jimmy did something wrong, there was swift punishment. "Jimmy says that he can remember six lickings that his father gave him," Jimmy's cousin Hugh remembered, "all with switches from a peach tree. If you've been switched with a sharp peach tree switch, you know you've gotten a licking and you're still smarting for hours."[7]

Jimmy earned the nickname "Hot," short for "Hotshot," because he knew how to make money. When he was just five years old, he went into the peanut fields to pull up peanuts. He boiled the peanuts and put them in half-pound bags. Jimmy pulled the bags to town in his wagon and sold them for five cents a bag. He made about a dollar a day. That was as much as many grown farmhands made at the time.

At 4:00 A.M., a clanging bell would start the day on the farm. The Carters and their farmhands headed for the fields in mule-drawn wagons. Some of the jobs were awful. Jimmy had to "mop cotton," which meant mixing molasses, water, and arsenic into a poisonous mess. Then Jimmy mopped each stalk of cotton to protect it against the boll weevil, a cotton pest.[8]

Jimmy was active in the local Baptist Church. He was also a good student. He was a friendly first-grader who always stuck out his hand and said "Hello, I'm

Carter with his father James Earl, Sr., and sisters Ruth (middle) and Gloria. Carter's father was very strict with him.

Jimmy Carter," when he met a stranger.[9] Jimmy attended a small, all-white elementary school.

Jimmy's Uncle Tom Gordy was in the United States Navy. He sent the family colorful postcards from all over the world. When Jimmy was in fourth grade, he read about the world's oceans. He began to dream of being a sailor like his uncle Tom. Jimmy earned straight A's in everything but music.

Lillian Carter later remembered Jimmy as "just a little redheaded, freckle-faced boy who lived in the country. There was nothing outstanding about Jimmy at all."[10] There was someone in Plains who did believe that Jimmy stood out. Miss Julia Coleman, a teacher, took an interest in promising children. She gave out silver stars to students who read five books and gold stars to those who read ten books. Jimmy promised to read *War and Peace* for her even though he was surprised to find it had almost fifteen hundred pages.[11] Coleman urged her students to memorize poems and recite them before the class.

Later, Jimmy Carter said of Coleman, ". . . she saw something in me, I think, when I was a little child, a hunger to learn. . . . she made sure that I listened to classical music. And she'd make sure that I learned the famous paintings."[12] Carter said that Coleman was one of two women who changed his life. The other was his mother.[13]

When he was fourteen, Jimmy wrote a letter to the United States Naval Academy. He asked how to enter. He was a very good student at Plains High School. He earned A's in every subject except physical education.

But Plains High School did not teach enough science and mathematics, so the Naval Academy at Annapolis turned Jimmy down. He could not enter Annapolis from high school.

Jimmy was the outstanding high school graduate at Plains High School in 1941. To prepare for Annapolis, he attended Southwestern Junior College in Americus, Georgia. Even there, the science and mathematics classes were poor. The educational system in these schools during the 1930s and 1940s lacked enough money to afford teachers for advanced classes. Carter's experience at these schools gave him a lifelong desire to improve education.

Carter left the junior college in 1942 and entered the Georgia Institute of Technology in Atlanta. Finally he had classes that would help him at Annapolis. He took mathematics and engineering and worked hard to catch up.

Although Carter was not a class leader, he was active in college life. Though not tall, he played basketball. He took part in calisthenics, body-building exercises. He went to parties and dated. He cheered for the college football team.

In the summer of 1943, Carter went to Annapolis. He was almost nineteen years old. Carter was five feet six inches tall, and he weighed less than 130 pounds. He and the other young men expected to be trained as naval officers who would play a part in winning World War II. He was finally ready to begin his naval career.

3

MARRIAGE AND THE UNITED STATES NAVY

Jimmy Carter entered Annapolis as a freshman, or plebe. The worst part of being a plebe was hazing—upperclassmen making life hard. For example, plebes could not sit at the table to eat. They had to eat under the table.

One night, a group of upperclassmen surrounded Carter. They ordered him to sing "Marching Through Georgia." This was the Union Civil War song Georgians hated. It was the song Union soldiers had sung as they marched through Georgia, burning many towns. The upperclassmen knew Carter was from Georgia. Because Carter refused to sing the song, his hazing got even worse. Carter held his ground and stuck it out.

The following summer, 1944, was much better. Carter was finally going to sea. World War II was going on, but Carter was not sent into action. He was given duty aboard a very old battleship—the USS *New York*. Carter and the other midshipmen (Naval training students) sailed down the east coast of the United States and in the Caribbean. One of Carter's jobs on the ship was cleaning the "after-head"—the toilet in the rear of the ship. His other job was manning a battle station where he operated a 45 millimeter antiaircraft battery (a cluster of heavy guns). Carter did not get the chance to fire those guns, because the USS *New York* did not go into battle.

One day, the ship's crew thought they saw a German submarine coming through the water at high speed. The USS *New York* turned sharply to avoid the submarine. In the middle of this violent maneuver, a part of the USS *New York* broke off, causing the old ship to shake. The crew was not sure what happened. Maybe they had been hit by a German torpedo, or perhaps they bumped into a reef. When the ship returned to port, Carter and the other midshipmen received combat ribbons.

The year 1945 was a good one for Carter at Annapolis. He learned how to fly and was doing well in his studies. In the summer, Carter returned to Plains to see his family. There was about to be a big change in Carter's life.

Rosalynn Smith, like Jimmy Carter, grew up in Plains. Because Plains was such a small town, they knew each other. Rosalynn was three years younger than Carter, so they were not friends.

However, Rosalynn was a friend of Jimmy Carter's younger sister, Ruth. When Rosalynn was thirteen, her father, Edgar Smith, grew very ill with leukemia. Lillian Carter went to the Smith house to help care for him until his death.

Jimmy Carter thought of Rosalynn Smith as his sister's little friend. Ruth Carter was very proud of her big brother. She proudly hung a picture of him in his naval uniform on the bedroom wall. This picture caught the eye of Rosalynn Smith, sixteen years old in the summer of 1945. "I thought he was the most handsome young man I had ever seen,"[1] she later said. She had been admiring Carter for a long time, but she said he seemed "so glamorous and out of reach."[2] The Carter family owned a store and hundreds of acres of land. Rosalynn Smith's mother, Allie Smith, was a poor widow with four children. She supported her family sewing bridal gowns and jackets.

Carter went out with a friend one summer night. He saw his sister and Rosalynn Smith walking down the street. He invited them both to a party in town. Smith fell in love with the young man in the midshipman's handsome white uniform. Carter did not notice her at all.[3]

The summer passed and Carter was about to return to Annapolis. He wanted to take a girl to the movies. He later described what happened. ". . . I was driving by the Plains Methodist Church and a young girl, who was quite a bit younger than I was, was in front of the

Carter turned this photo of himself in his midshipman's uniform into one of the many love letters he sent Rosalynn Smith in 1945.

church and I was looking for a blind date to go to a movie. . . . as I couldn't find any older girl to go with me, I asked her for a date. When I got home that night I went in to see my mother." Carter told his mother that he liked Rosalynn Smith and "She's the one I want to marry."[4] Carter was twenty and Smith had just turned seventeen. She was a student at Southwestern Junior College. She wanted to go on to the university and become an interior decorator.

Carter returned to Annapolis and wrote Smith letters every other day. She answered them all. When Carter came home for Christmas, he proposed marriage and she said no. Smith loved Carter, but she wanted to think about her future a little longer. She was not sure if she wanted to give up her education and career.

In February 1946, Carter again asked Smith to marry him. This time she had made up her mind. She agreed. In June 1946, Carter graduated from the United States Naval Academy at Annapolis. He was fifty-ninth in a class of eight hundred. That put him in the top 10 percent of his class.

Carter's mother and Rosalynn Smith stood on either side of Carter to snap the Ensign bars onto his shoulders. On July 7, 1946, Rosalynn Smith and Jimmy Carter were married at the Plains Methodist Church. Then Rosalynn Carter joined the Baptist Church where the Carter family worshipped as a gesture of unity.

The Carters began their married life in Norfolk, Virginia. Carter started his naval career on two experimental gunnery ships, the *Wyoming* and the *Mississippi.* The ships were floating laboratories for testing new electronics and photography on weapons. Carter was one of the officers in charge. Rosalynn Carter was home alone much of the time during the first two years of their marriage. Carter was at sea Monday through Friday.

In July 1947, the Carters' first child was born. He was named John William Carter and nicknamed Jack.

Jimmy Carter decided to enter the submarine branch of the Navy. For young officers looking for

Rosalynn Smith and Lillian Carter attach Ensign bars to Carter's shoulders upon his graduation from the U.S. Naval Academy in June 1946. Only a month later, Carter and Smith would be married.

promotion, it was a good place to be. The training was hard and dangerous. Only the best officers were wanted. Carter studied submarine systems and took part in long underwater training. Mock battles were staged. In December 1948, Lieutenant Carter finished submarine school.

The Carters returned to Plains for Christmas. Carter had an exciting new assignment. He would be an officer on the USS *Pomfret,* a submarine. The Carters would be stationed in Hawaii. First, Carter had to take a three-month tour of duty to China. Rosalynn Carter and little Jack would stay in Plains, then join Carter at Pearl Harbor in Hawaii.

Lieutenant Carter joined the crew of the USS *Pomfret.* Soon the submarine ran into a fierce five-day storm at sea. The submarine came to the surface to recharge its batteries. Carter stood night watch on the bridge of the submarine, about fifteen feet above the water. Suddenly, a huge storm-driven wave swept over Carter. Water surged six feet over his head. The power of the water pulled Carter's hand from the railing. He was swept into the sea. He was swimming inside a churning wave. The next wave tossed Carter back onto the barrel of the gun. Clinging to the gun barrel, Carter was able to lower himself down and scramble back on deck. It had been a dangerous moment. Carter had almost drowned.

The storm had knocked out the USS *Pomfret*'s radio. They could receive messages but they could not send

Carter had reached the rank of lieutenant by the time he was working on the submarine USS Pomfret.

them. After a few days of hearing nothing from the submarine, the Navy feared the USS *Pomfret* had sunk. Aboard the submarine, the crew heard this message: "To all ships in the Pacific: Be on the lookout for floating debris left by submarine USS *Pomfret*, believed to have been sunk approximately seven hundred miles south of Midway Island."[5]

The wives of the crew already in Hawaii heard the bad news. Rosalynn Carter back in Plains did not. She found out what happened when she met her husband in Hawaii and he told her.[6]

The Carters had a pleasant year and a half in Hawaii. They both fell in love with the tropical island.[7] Jimmy Carter learned to play the ukelele. The Carters' second son, James Earl Carter, III, nicknamed Chip, was born in April 1950.

That same year, the Korean War broke out. The USS *Pomfret* was ordered back to the United States. Carter became a senior officer on the Navy's first postwar submarine, the USS *K-1*. It was an experimental submarine not yet launched. The USS *K-1* was a submarine killer. It was made to find and destroy enemy submarines.

The Carters were stationed in San Diego, California. Housing in good neighborhoods was too expensive for the young naval officer, so Rosalynn Carter found herself in a run-down neighborhood with a high crime rate. She put empty ice-cube trays on the window sills so she would be warned if someone was trying to break in. It was a hard place to live with small children.

When the *K-1* was almost completed, the Carters were sent to New London, Connecticut. Carter was promoted to the rank of full lieutenant from junior grade. He became the junior officer in charge of engineering on the *K-1*.

Carter wanted to join the Atomic Division of the Bureau of Ships, headed by Captain Hyman Rickover. He was called to Washington, where Rickover questioned him. Rickover asked Carter many tough questions. Then he asked Carter if he had done his best at Annapolis. Carter admitted that he had not always done his best. Rickover asked why he had not, and Carter had no good answer. Still, he was given the job.[8] He joined the crew of the new atomic submarine, USS *Seawolf.* Rickover later became an admiral. He played a major role in the creation of atomic submarines for the United States. Admiral Rickover became one of Carter's heroes.[9]

The Carters' third son, Donnel Jeffrey, nicknamed Jeff, was born in 1952. The family moved to Schenectady, New York. Carter went to graduate school at Union College. He taught physics and other courses to the crew of the USS *Seawolf.* Carter's career was going well. But there was tragic news from Plains that would change his life forever.

4

HOME to PLAINS AND POLITICS

Earl Carter, Jimmy's father, was dying of cancer. The family hurried home to Plains. Earl Carter had just been elected to the Georgia State Legislature before he became ill. His store and his farm were doing well. When Jimmy Carter heard about his father's illness, he felt sad about having been away from home for the past eleven years. He needed to spend time with his father now.[1]

While in Plains, Jimmy Carter learned things about his father he never knew before. Earl Carter loaned money to poor people. He also helped support widows. He even bought graduation dresses for high school girls too poor to afford them. Carter admired the life his father led. Suddenly, living that kind of life looked better than a naval career.

28

"I had only one life to live, and I wanted to live it as a civilian, with a potentially fuller opportunity for varied public service," Carter said.[2] Carter resigned from the Navy.

Rosalynn Carter was very unhappy about this decision. She liked being a Navy wife. She enjoyed living away from Plains. "I argued. I cried. I even screamed at him," she said. "I loved our life in the Navy, and the independence I had finally achieved. I knew it would be gone if we went home to live in the same community with my mother and Jimmy's mother. Plains had too many ghosts for me."[3]

Still, the Carters did move back to Plains. Earl Carter died in July 1953. Jimmy Carter promptly joined all the organizations to which his father had belonged. He served on the hospital, school, and library boards. Jimmy Carter even bought graduation dresses for poor high school girls as his father had done before him. "It was almost as if Uncle Earl was guiding his son from on high, the way Jimmy did everything he could to follow in his father's footsteps," cousin Hugh Carter said.[4]

The first year back in Plains was very hard. A drought ruined Georgia's peanut crop. Carter had never run a business before, and he made mistakes. The Carters lived on about $200 that first year.[5] Carter worked hard in the office as well as doing farm labor. A neighbor said, "Jimmy could do more work than any other three men put together."[6]

In the spring of 1955, Rosalynn Carter took over the office of the peanut business. This helped improve things. She was good at managing the business. Also that year, the rains came. Soon peanuts were pouring into the Carter warehouse. The family moved from an apartment to a big house. The Carter boys had a horse and dogs. Life got better, and the Carters took camping trips and fished in Florida.

In 1954, life all over the South was changed by a Supreme Court ruling called *Brown* v. *Board of Education*. This ruling ordered desegregation of the schools. The Supreme Court ordered desegregation to proceed with all deliberate speed, but assigned the lower courts the responsibility of bringing it about. It was no longer permitted to segregate children according to color. Many white people in the South were angry about this. They decided to fight it. They formed White Citizens' Councils to stop integration of black and white children in public schools. In Plains, all the white men joined the White Citizens' Council—all but Jimmy Carter.

One day, the Constable of Plains came to see Carter. He asked him to join the White Citizens' Council. Carter refused. Then some neighbors came and told Carter he better join up. If he did not, he would lose all his customers. Nobody would buy peanuts from the Carter warehouse. Carter said, "I am not going to join the White Citizens' Council."[7] Soon there were threats against the Carters.[8]

The Carters had few friends in Plains they could talk to about integration. The Carters were willing to have black and white children go to school together, but their neighbors were not. One day, as the Carters returned from a school-board meeting, they found a hate message on the front of the peanut warehouse. "I knew how some people felt," Rosalynn Carter said, "but it was a shock to have it right there in front of me."[9] The Carters stood firm in their beliefs.

Jimmy Carter decided to do something else his father had done—run for public office. In 1962, Jimmy Carter ran for Georgia's State Senate. The whole Carter family joined the campaign. They talked to people and passed out leaflets about Jimmy Carter. On election night, it turned out that Carter won everywhere but in Quitman County. The vote against Carter in Quitman County was enough to have cost him the election. Friends came to Carter and told him that the vote in Quitman County had been dishonest. People had voted in public instead of in secret as they were supposed to do. Also, there were 330 voters registered in Quitman County, but 430 ballots were cast.

Carter refused to accept the vote results. He went to Quitman County to talk to the people. When he arrived, men followed him. There were threats. A man told Rosalynn Carter that the last person to stir up trouble in Quitman County had his businesses burned down.[10] Cousin Hugh Carter said, "I often think back about those days and how we could have been killed or severely beaten."[11] Rosalynn Carter said that she was scared and, "I think Jimmy was frightened too, but we didn't talk about it much."[12]

Jimmy Carter proved the election was dishonest, and he was elected to the Georgia State Senate. When he went off to Atlanta to serve his first term, his wife remembered the threats.[13] She left porch lights burning at night. She slept in the den with her children, with a sofa braced against the door.[14]

During his term in the State Senate, Carter worked to improve public education. In 1966, Carter decided to run for governor of Georgia. He ran in the Democratic primary against Lester Maddox. Maddox was in favor of racial segregation. Carter lost the election, and for a while he felt very sad. He often walked alone across the peanut fields, his shoulders hunched over, staring down at the ground or up at the sky.[15] He had worked so hard during the campaign that he had lost twenty pounds. He had borrowed money for the campaign and now he had to pay it back. Carter was in a low mood, but the spirits of the whole family rose in October 1967. Daughter Amy Lynn was born.

In 1970, Carter ran for governor again. Many young volunteers helped. Carter was better known this time, and he won the election. In January 1971, Carter became the sixty-seventh governor of Georgia. "I say to you . . . that the time for racial discrimination is over," Carter said.[16] He promised no more schools would be closed to African Americans.

Carter was a hard-working governor. He formed a special group to solve racial problems and set up a program to help drug addicts stop their habit. He reduced the number of state agencies from 300 to just 22. Business got done more quickly and more smoothly in Georgia.

Carter also helped improve the environment in Georgia. There was a plan to build a dam that would have damaged many acres of beautiful wilderness. Carter stopped it. He also improved the way judges were chosen. Before, judges had been chosen from among friends of important people. Carter chose judges with good legal backgrounds. It did not matter who their friends were.

While he was governor of Georgia, Carter increased the number of African-American state employees from 4,850 to 6,684. He improved services for people with mental illness by opening over one hundred new mental-health centers. Carter made it easier for Georgians to get help from the state government if they were victims of consumer fraud.

Carter was one of the new southern governors who came to office during the 1970s. They were a different kind of southern politician. They favored racial equality, and they promoted economic development. In May 1971, *Time* magazine described Carter as "Soft-voiced, assured, looking eerily like John Kennedy from certain angles."[17]

Carter saw politics as a way of living out his

personal beliefs. One of his favorite authors, Reinhold Niebuhr, put it this way, "The sad duty of politics is to establish justice in a sinful world."[18] Carter saw his political career as a chance to do good. He could serve God and humanity through political office.

One of the last things Carter did as governor of Georgia was to put a portrait of Dr. Martin Luther King, Jr., in the state capital. Not everyone liked this action. Members of the Ku Klux Klan, a white supremacist group that opposed integration, paraded outside the capital in protest as the picture was hung.

Many of Jimmy Carter's friends told him he was such

SOURCE DOCUMENT

'No, I Don't Think of Myself as a Carbon Copy of Kennedy. Rather, I Prefer to Think of Kennedy as a Rough Draft of Me!'

Because of his appearance and support of certain issues, Carter was often compared to former President John F. Kennedy.

a good governor that he would also make a good President of the United States. In fact, when Senator George McGovern became the Democratic candidate for President in 1972, Jimmy Carter's name came up as a possible choice for Vice President.

In September 1974, Jimmy Carter began to seriously consider running for President.

5

A RUN FOR THE WHITE HOUSE

Jimmy Carter met with the governors of the other twelve original American colonies in September 1974. It was the two hundredth anniversary of the First Continental Congress. The governors talked about leadership in America. Carter believed he could lead his country. In October, he told his family, "I am going to run for President of the United States."[1] Some family members asked him why he thought he could win. Carter said "he felt on safe ground and was just as qualified as [others who were running] for the office."[2]

The last American President from the Deep South (the region including Tennessee, the Carolinas, Georgia, Alabama, and Mississippi) had been Andrew Johnson from North Carolina in 1865. Johnson became

36

President only by first running as Abraham Lincoln's Vice President.

Carter was proud of his southern roots. "I'm proud being an American, but I'm even more proud being a Southerner!" he said.[3] Now he would have to convince the American people that he was the best man for the Democratic nomination. He set out to tell America that a southerner was just as capable of being President as any other person.[4]

In December 1974, Carter publicly announced his plans to run for President. He spoke from the Civic Center in Atlanta. He knew he was not well known outside Georgia. Carter said, "Our strategy was simple: make a total effort all over the nation."[5]

Carter promised tax and welfare reform. He promised a strong national defense. He promised his government would be open. The private rights of all Americans would be respected. Above all, he would be honest. This was a big issue in the United States. Just a few months before Carter announced he would run for President, President Richard Nixon had to resign from office. Nixon was facing impeachment because he was involved in covering up a burglary at Democratic National Headquarters in the Watergate Hotel. This was called the Watergate scandal.

Carter's campaign workers were called the Peanut Brigade. Many of them were young people who had worked for Carter in Georgia. Now they went all over America, often door-to-door, talking about Jimmy

Carter. Carter and his family campaigned all over the country. Jimmy Carter personally covered about five hundred thousand miles.

During the campaign, "Mr. Peanut" often appeared. This was the world's largest man-made peanut. It was made from hoops, chicken wire, foil, and foam rubber. It was 14 feet high and weighed four hundred and fifty pounds. "Mr. Peanut" stood behind Carter during a speech in Evansville, Indiana, and then became one of the props that Carter used to get people to stop and listen.[6]

Carter told friends at the start of the campaign, "You probably think I'm crazy but I'm going to be the next President of the United States."[7] His confidence inspired people to climb on the bandwagon. More and more people were taking a look at Jimmy Carter and what he had to offer.

In 1976, many prominent Democrats were also running for President. Washington Senator Henry Jackson, Texas Senator Lloyd Bentsen, and California Governor Jerry Brown were among them. To win the Democratic nomination, Carter had to beat the others in primary elections. These are elections where Democrats and Republicans choose their candidates.

Carter lost some states like Alabama, Nebraska, Oregon, Idaho, Nevada, Maryland, and California. He won in New Hampshire, Georgia, Texas, Indiana, Florida, and Ohio, among others. When the Democratic convention was held in New York City in July, Jimmy

Carter won on the first ballot. He was chosen to be the Democratic candidate for President. Carter chose Minnesota Senator Walter "Fritz" Mondale to be his vice-presidential running mate.

Carter would run against incumbent Republican President Gerald Ford. Ford had become President in August 1974, when President Richard Nixon resigned.

Carter campaigned for President as an average man just trying to do his best. "I have never desired to be better or wiser than any other person," he said.[8] That was a breath of fresh air to many people.

During the campaign, Carter was interviewed about his personal life. There was so little known about him that people were anxious for details. Carter said that for relaxation he read books, hunted for arrowheads, and walked for hours in the woods.[9] He also discussed his religious beliefs. He said he was a "born-again Christian." He explained that, as an adult, he had decided to have a close, personal relationship with Jesus Christ. He said he prayed half a dozen times a day, though he was not praying to win the election. He just prayed to do his best.[10]

Carter discussed his ideas about justice. He wanted the police to spend most of their time looking for violent criminals. He wanted drug addicts and alcoholics to be helped, not sent to jail.[11] When asked if he feared being assassinated like Presidents Abraham Lincoln and John Kennedy, Carter said, "I'm not afraid of death. . . . It's part of my religious belief. I just look at death as not a

SOURCE DOCUMENT

THE WHITE HOUSE

WASHINGTON

April 21, 1978

Stu —
Read my Law Day
Speech — The justice
System still stinks
J
p.s. lawyers don't
see it my way,
I know

MEMORANDUM FOR: THE PRESIDENT

FROM: STU EIZENSTAT *Stu*

SUBJECT: Justice Speech

Since Judge Bell's memorandum on the crime speech was written, additional work has gone forward in planning such a speech. First, of course, a forum has been selected -- the 100th anniversary of the Los Angeles Bar Association, which you are scheduled to address on May 4. Second, Judge Bell, OMB and I agree that your speech should not focus on crime as much as it does on the broader subject of justice. We believe that you can use this occasion, the 4th anniversary of your Law Day speech in Georgia, to give a stirring address on the subject of justice in America.

That speech would not only follow-through on the themes emphasized in your earlier Law Day speech, but would also state what your Administration has done to date and what it plans to do in the civil liberties and criminal justice areas. We do not want the speech to be a laundry list of everything the Administration has done or is doing in these areas, but we do think that you should emphasize and take credit for some of our very positive initiatives. These include the general outlines of the LEAA reorganization, criminal code reform, the wiretap legislation, the intelligence agency Executive Order and the improved access to courts proposals. We believe that the overriding impression the audience should receive from your speech is not so much the number and variety of improvements to be proposed, but rather the depth of your commitment to justice for all Americans and protection of Constitutional guarantees and freedoms. To a large extent the speech can be seen as a domestic human rights address -- an attempt to indicate that your concern about human rights begins at home and is being met regularly by your Administration's efforts in the civil liberties and criminal justice areas.

This memo, written by Stu Eizenstadt, shows Carter's continued interest in American justice after he gained the presidency.

threat. It's inevitable and I have an assurance of eternal life."[12]

During the televised Carter-Ford debate in 1976, the main issue was the economy. America was in a recession and many people were out of work. Another issue was former President Richard Nixon. Many believed Nixon had broken the law when he was President, and he should have been tried in a court. President Ford had pardoned Nixon so he would not be put on trial. Ford believed a trial of a former President would be bad for the United States. However, some Americans held Nixon's pardon against Ford.

On November 2, 1976, Jimmy Carter won a very close election. Carter received almost 41 million votes, and Ford received somewhat more than 39 million. Carter won 297 electoral votes to Ford's 240.

Jimmy Carter was President-elect of the United States, and he returned to Plains to thank all of his friends for helping him win. "I think the sun's rising on a beautiful new day. A beautiful new spirit in this country. A beautiful new commitment to the future. I feel good about it," Carter said. "And I love [every one] of you and I thank you for it."[13]

On January 20, 1977, thousands watched in person and millions more on television as Jimmy Carter was sworn in as the thirty-ninth President of the United States. Yet there was something unusual about this Inauguration Day. Before this, it was customary for the President-elect and his family to ride in a big limousine or carriage. However, on this day, Carter ordered the limousine to halt. Carter and his family got out and stepped into the street.

The Carters began to walk down the center of the broad avenue. Jimmy and Rosalynn Carter, with daughter Amy between them, led the way. They were followed by the three Carter sons and their wives. The Carters did this on purpose. Carter wanted to show all Americans that the new President was just an ordinary man. He wanted to be one of them. Riding in the limousine appeared to put him above the crowd.

Carter recalled the reactions of the crowd. "Some of them wept openly, and when I saw this, a few tears of joy ran down my cold cheeks. It was one of those few perfect moments in life when everything seems absolutely right."[14]

At last, the new President reached the place where he would give his inaugural address. He put a lot of work into what he planned to say. He had studied speeches of previous Presidents and resolved to be brief. Carter wanted to say something that would really be important to Americans.

President Carter promised to uphold human rights so people all over the world would be treated fairly. He pledged to keep America's environment clean and beautiful. Carter then talked about something very dear to his heart. "We will move this year a step toward our ultimate goal—the elimination of all nuclear weapons from this earth."[15]

Instead of taking a limousine, Carter and his family decided to walk to the site of his inaugural address. Carter believed that taking a limousine would make him appear better than the American people.

When Carter finished taking his oath of office, a chorus from Atlanta's various colleges, including Morehouse College, sang "The Battle Hymn of the Republic." Carter had received an honorary degree from the African-American Morehouse College. Once, an angry white man asked Carter if he really had accepted a degree from this African-American college. "Yes," Carter said, "I'm going to be the first Morehouse boy in the White House."[16] This is just what happened.

6

A DOMESTIC AGENDA

After Jimmy Carter became President, there were "hillbilly" jokes made about him. Because he came from a small southern town and was a farmer, he was ridiculed. Even though Carter's parents were educated, successful people, and Carter had graduated from Annapolis, some people looked down on the Carters because of the region they came from.

Republican Senator Barry Goldwater, Jr., joked that when the Carters moved into the White House, they would plow up the lawn for this year's "peanut, 'tater, and cone pone [corn used to make cornbread—a southern staple] crop."[1] There were jokes about Carter's clothing. People said his jackets were too big, his trousers were too short, and he wore farmer's shoes.[2]

Carter had run for President calling himself an

"outsider" who would clean up the mess the insiders had made. Now, as President, he was living in Washington, D.C., and he had to work with those insiders—the men and women of Congress.

Usually when someone becomes President there is a period called a "honeymoon" when relations are friendly between the President and Congress. Bills get passed more smoothly during this period. Carter's honeymoon was very short even though both the House of Representatives and the Senate were controlled by Democrats. Carter, a Democrat, should have had good relations with Congress, yet this was not the case.

One reason for the difficulties Carter had was that he was a moderate, not a liberal, Democrat. Liberal Democrats want to spend a lot of money to solve problems. They favor bigger social programs for education, health, and welfare. Carter, however, was worried about too much government spending. The United States owed a lot of money—called the national debt. Carter wanted to reduce the national debt. Liberal Democrats disliked Carter from the beginning. House majority leader Thomas "Tip" O'Neill of Massachusetts had been a powerful liberal Democrat for many years. He accused Carter of turning against the programs the Democrats had always supported.[3]

Another problem Carter had was lack of experience as an elected official in Washington. Many of his close aides were unfamiliar with Washington politics, too. Like Carter, they were from Georgia. Carter was

SOURCE DOCUMENT

THE WHITE HOUSE

WASHINGTON

3-10-77

To Sen Humphrey

Thank you for your strong & effective support of Paul Warnke.

I believe this action will pay rich dividends for us all.

This help is typical of your sound judgment & leadership ability.

Your friend

Jimmy

Despite oftentimes bad relations with Congress, Carter had his supporters. Here, he thanks Senator Hubert Humphrey of Minnesota.

"intensely loyal only to his close friends from Georgia."[4] So neither Carter nor his aides had a good idea about how Washington worked.

President Carter's chief of staff, Jack Watson, warned the President not to take on too much work personally. Watson didn't want Carter buried in too many details that could be handled by others.[5] Carter started out working about fifty-five hours a week. Soon he was working eighty hours a week, double the average work week.[6]

As governor of Georgia, Carter had eliminated many agencies that were not needed. He wanted to do the same thing in Washington. He met with Democratic Representative Jack Brooks of Texas. Brooks headed the important Government Operations Committee. Any bill to reorganize the federal government had to go through his committee first. "I did not make any progress with Jack Brooks," Carter later admitted.[7]

When Carter began trying to cut government spending, he got more support from Republicans than Democrats. He wanted to cut out some "pork barrel" bills. These are projects like dams or public buildings built mostly to create jobs. A congressperson sometimes will write a "pork barrel" bill to create more jobs in his or her district. This is popular with the voters of that district. It helps the person get reelected to Congress. Yet each year hundreds of these "pork barrel" bills cost the federal government a lot of money. They raise the national debt. Carter tried to cut out some of them, but

Congress blocked him. Carter could not do in Washington what he had done in Georgia. He could just make a few small changes.

Carter next turned to the problem of medical costs. He promised the voters he would keep down soaring medical costs. In 1970, a single person paid about $12 a month for medical insurance. By 1976, when Carter was elected, this had risen to about $30 a month. Many Americans could no longer afford health insurance. Carter tried to keep his promise, but he ran into opposition from strong hospital and medical lobbies. Lobbies are groups that try to protect the special interests of various industries. Carter described the power of these lobbies as "almost unbelievable."[8] He lost his fight to control the cost of medical insurance. In 1981, when Carter left office, a single person was paying $42 a month for health insurance. Seven years later, in 1988, the bill had risen to $88 a month.[9]

Energy was also a big problem in 1977. Americans were using too much of it. They were especially using too much oil from Middle East countries. There was often trouble in that part of the world. Oil was sometimes cut off, or prices rose very rapidly. Carter wanted to give the United States a new energy policy.

When Carter spoke to the American people about this, he was sitting by a fireplace and wearing a cardigan sweater. The message was to turn off the gas, use renewable resources like wood, and wear warm clothing. Carter announced a new cabinet-level agency—the

Sitting by the White House fireplace, Carter announced his new energy policy, which included use of wood fuel over gas, as well as the establishment of the Department of Energy.

United States Department of Energy. It would make plans for new energy sources. It would also help Americans find ways to save the resources that they had. Now Carter had a new fight on his hands. The automobile and oil lobbies did not like his message. Carter wanted new automobiles to burn less fuel, but that meant making major changes in automotive design. On October 15, 1978, after an eighteen-month struggle with Congress, Carter's energy bills finally passed both houses.

"The most important factor is that the attitude of the American people [concerning energy] has changed,"

Carter lost some popularity because of his announcement of his energy plan. This loss came mainly from the automobile and oil industries, while most of the American public was receptive to the new energy policies.

President Carter said.[10] There would now be new laws providing for the manufacture of cars that got more miles per gallon of fuel. New fuels would be developed. Carter helped people see that conservation needs to be a way of life. All over America, people were turning out lights in unused rooms. They were turning down the heat and putting on extra sweaters. As one article put it, "Carter's close-to-people style is paying off big."[11]

When asked in November 1978 what he had learned so far about Washington, Carter described two nasty surprises. One was how long it took to get a bill through Congress. The other was the "irresponsibility of the press."[12] Some of Carter's bitterness against the press came from the Bert Lance incident.

Bert Lance was a small-town banker from Georgia, a close personal friend of Carter. When Carter became President, he named Lance director of the White House Office of Management and Budget (OMB). This office helps the President to prepare and administer the budget. Lance had to be approved by the Senate before he could take the OMB job. That is where the trouble began. The senators looked into Lance's career as a Georgia banker. Lance had been careless with paperwork, and he had given loans to friends and neighbors in a casual way. This was not unusual for a small-town Georgia banker. But soon there were charges of wrongdoing against Lance.

Accusations against Lance flew from every newspaper and television station. Every detail of his life

SOURCE DOCUMENT

STATEMENT BY THE PRESIDENT

I have decided to sign S. 233, which authorizes appropriations for the United States Travel Service.

At the beginning of the year I recommended that the Service be eliminated, for its function can and should be performed by the private sector. I have not changed my view.

I have signed S. 233, however, because the appropriations for the Travel Service have already been enacted as part of a separate bill. I will work to restructure the Federal Government's travel program in order to conform its operation with what I believe to be an appropriate Federal role in tourism promotion.

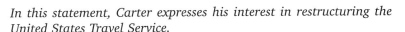

In this statement, Carter expresses his interest in restructuring the United States Travel Service.

was examined. New stories of things he might have done wrong came out each day. Carter admitted that it was impossible to "overestimate the damage" that was done to his administration because of the Lance incident.[13] Carter had promised an honest government, and when people heard these charges, they lost some faith in him. The Lance case rubbed the shine from the "clean government image that Mr. Carter had so carefully fashioned."[14]

Bert Lance insisted he had done nothing wrong. He said he just loaned money to people he trusted and did not cheat anyone. Still, the whole country seemed to turn against him. On September 20, 1977, he quit as OMB director. Even after Lance left, the charges against him continued. Lance eventually spent about one million dollars trying to clear his name.

During his presidency, Jimmy Carter's domestic agenda included deep concern for the environment. He

The extended First Family—standing left to right: Annette, Jeff, Chip, Allie M. Smith, Carter, Amy, Jason, Rosalynn, Jack, Judy, Sarah; seated: James, Lillian.

enlarged the National Park System to include 103 million acres of Alaskan wilderness. Carter also worked hard on another issue he cared deeply about—human rights. He tried to build his foreign policy on the principle of advancing the cause of human rights around the world.

7

HUMAN RIGHTS AND PANAMA

President Carter wanted the United States to stand for "basic human rights and freedom."[1] Whenever he heard of people in a foreign country being persecuted, he wanted to do something. In 1977, Russian scientist Andrei Sakharov was arrested by the Soviet police because he spoke out for freedom. Sakharov sent a message to Carter asking for help. Carter promised Sakharov he would speak out against injustice in the Soviet Union, and he did. Although Sakharov was not freed for several years, he continued to have great respect for Carter and his commitment to human rights.[2]

The leaders of the Soviet Union were angry about the Sakharov incident. They said that how they treated their own citizens was none of America's business. *U.S.*

56

News and World Report wondered whether Carter wanted the United States to be the "Moral Policeman of the World?"[3] Nonetheless, Carter stuck to his policy.

In the Soviet Union, there were many Jews who wanted to leave. Carter put pressure on the Soviet Union to let them go. In 1976, the year before Carter took office, only about fourteen thousand Jews were allowed to leave. After Carter's pressure in 1979, over fifty thousand Jews were allowed to leave. Thousands of political prisoners all over the world were freed because of Carter's efforts. Still, Carter's interference was often criticized by German and other European leaders as bad foreign policy.[4]

Carter's National Security Advisor, Zbigniew Brzezinski (zuh-bihg-nehf breh-zihn-skih), said great progress in human rights was made. He admitted, however, that it is easier to pressure a small country to treat its people better than it is to put pressure on a large country.[5]

When Carter was governor of Georgia, his wife Rosalynn played a large role. She worked at a mental hospital to learn more about the problems of mental illness. Now that she was America's first lady, she continued her active role. Rosalynn Carter not only helped her husband by her gracious presence in his dealings with foreign leaders, but she spent a lot of time on special projects of her own. She visited nursing homes to better understand the problems of the elderly. She urged better prenatal care for poor women and

Jimmy and Rosalynn Carter pose in the White House in 1977. Rosalynn Carter was an active First Lady, working on many special projects of her own.

helped develop programs to find meaningful jobs for the mentally challenged.[6]

Soon after becoming President in 1977, Carter pardoned ten thousand young American men who had evaded the draft during the Vietnam War (1957–1975). Some people did not like this decision. Still, Carter wanted to put a stop to problems regarding the Vietnam War that were dividing America. In the early months of 1977, Carter also began work on the Panama Canal problem.

In the early 1900s, the United States wanted to build a canal in Central America between the Atlantic and Pacific oceans. At the time, ships going from one coast of the United States to the other had to go all the way around the tip of South America. It took about six months to make that journey. Building a canal would cut this time in half.

The place where the United States wanted to build the canal was owned by the South American country of Colombia. Colombia refused to allow the United States to build the canal. In 1903, President Theodore Roosevelt had helped the Panamanian people who lived in that part of Colombia revolt against Colombia. Panama then became an independent country. Panama had agreed to let the United States build the canal. The canal was finished in 1914. The land around the canal, called the Canal Zone, was rented from Panama. The United States ran the canal.

In time, the Panamanian people began to want more

SOURCE DOCUMENT

THE PRESIDENT HAS SEEN.

THE WHITE HOUSE
WASHINGTON

March 9, 1977

*Jim
see me.
after I look
over st & nsc
1st drafts –
J*

MEMO FOR THE PRESIDENT

FROM JIM FALLOWS *JF*

SUBJECT: UN SPEECH

There is a draft of this speech in the works at the NSC. The State Department has also sent its suggestions over to the NSC. I've seen none of these versions, and I have not come across anyone who has a very clear understanding of just what emphases <u>you</u> want in the speech.

Because we are on a tight schedule (I will apparently not see Dr. Brzezinski's version until Friday), I would be very grateful if you could briefly outline the points and the tone you want to have in the speech. Thanks very much.

*Major thrusts of our foreign policy –
Check Campaign speeches. SALT. Non Prolif.
N/s – Support of UN – Economic –
Human Rights. Ease tensions (travel, etc)
Recognize aspirations of LDC's. Basic
issues in Panama, E Medit, S Africa,
M East
Brief. not > 30 min. E slow delivery.*

J. C.

In a memo from Jim Fallows to Carter, we get a behind-the-scenes look at a presidential speech. In Carter's comments, we see his intention to talk about issues in Panama.

control over the Panama Canal. In 1963, the Panamanian flag flew side by side with the American flag. Yet the Panamanians wanted full control of the canal.

In 1974, Carter said he believed the Panama Canal should belong to Panama. Most Americans did not agree. They argued that since the United States built the canal, it was ours. A 1975 poll taken on the issue revealed that most Americans wanted to keep the canal.

In 1977, Carter began talks with Panama's leaders. A new treaty was agreed upon, giving Panama control of the Canal Zone. Panama and the United States would run the canal together until the year 2000. At that time, United States military forces would leave. The Panama Canal would then belong to Panama, but if a foreign power attacked the canal, the United States could defend it.

The United States Senate had to approve this treaty by a two-thirds vote. Almost 80 percent of the people in the United States opposed this treaty. It would be very hard for Carter to sell such an unpopular treaty to the Senate. Enemies of the treaty accused Carter of giving away a canal that belonged to the United States.[7] Senators feared they would not be reelected if they supported the treaty.

Carter worked hard to win over undecided senators. He spent hours talking to them and taking them to lunch. On April 18, 1978, the Senate approved the treaty 67 to 43 without a single vote to spare. Carter thanked all the senators who voted for the treaty even though it might cost them their jobs. In fact, many of those senators did lose their jobs—and their political careers. Twenty-one of the senators who supported Carter on the treaty did not return to the Senate. They either were defeated for reelection, or they did not even run for reelection. Voters who opposed the treaty had turned against them.

For Carter, it was a hard-won victory. He wanted good relations with Latin America. He believed the new Panama Canal treaty would help. Venezuelan President Carlos Andres Pérez said the treaty was the "most significant advance in political affairs in the Western Hemisphere in this century."[8]

Carter also wanted good relations with China and a reduction in nuclear weapons so the world would be safer. More fights with Congress lay ahead.

8

CHINA, SALT, AND STORM OVER IRAN

I n 1949, the Communist People's Republic of China was formed. There had been a long civil war in China between the Communists and the Nationalists, who were non-Communist. The United States supported the Nationalists. When the Communists won, the Nationalist leaders moved to nearby Taiwan, an island off China. They set up a democratic government there and called it the true government of China. They said the Communist government that controlled most of China was illegal.

For almost twenty-five years, the United States ignored the People's Republic of China, recognizing Taiwan as China. The United States had no diplomatic relations with the People's Republic of China, commonly called Red China.

In 1972, then President Richard Nixon visited China and talked to the Communist leaders. It was a first step in having normal diplomatic relations with the country. In 1973, there was some diplomatic contact between the United States and China. Jimmy Carter, however, wanted to develop full diplomatic relations between the United States and the People's Republic of China. He also wanted to make sure the peace and safety of the people on Taiwan were protected.[1]

In November 1978, talks began between the United States and the People's Republic of China. In December, an agreement was reached, formally recognizing the People's Republic of China as the sole legal government

A handshake with China's Deputy Premier Deng Xiaoping affirms the American-Chinese accord to establish full diplomatic relations.

of China. The United States established diplomatic relations with the People's Republic of China, effective January 1, 1979. Diplomatic relations with Taiwan were cut, but unofficial ties and aid to Taiwan continued.

Carter wanted to reduce the number of nuclear weapons in the world through the Strategic Arms Limitation Talks (SALT). Both the United States and the Soviet Union would agree to cut down their number of nuclear weapons. A similar treaty, SALT I, had been agreed to in 1972. Some nuclear weapons had been cut back. Carter hoped SALT II would move the process even further along.

In September 1978, a SALT II Treaty was written. It then had to be approved by the United States Senate. Carter had another big battle on his hands because many senators had bitter feelings toward the Soviet Union. He tried to convince senators that if the treaty were not approved, the rest of the world would look at the United States as a nation of "warmongers."[2]

As the fight over the SALT II Treaty went on in the Senate, Carter's leadership came under fire. One critic said, "Jimmy Carter was not a majestic personal figure like [Franklin] Roosevelt and he doesn't inspire fear like [Lyndon] Johnson." The critic added, "to govern properly, a president must generate a respect bordering on fear."[3] Another critic said, "Jimmy Carter did not get us into the troubles, but he has not gotten us out, either. And that was the job he said he wanted—to set things right—and it was the job we elected him to do."[4]

Despite this signing of the SALT II agreement by Carter and Russian President Leonid Brezhnev, the treaty was never approved by the Senate. This was due to the Soviet invasion of Afghanistan.

In December 1979, Soviet troops invaded Afghanistan to help a pro-Communist faction overthrow the government. This ended all hope of the SALT II Treaty being approved. Strong anti-Soviet feeling spread all over the United States. Congress refused to even talk about a treaty with the Soviet Union.

Because of the Soviet invasion of Afghanistan, Carter took other actions against the Soviet Union. He stopped the sale of grain to them. The 1980 summer Olympic games were to be held in Moscow, and Carter told American athletes to stay home. The 1980 summer Olympics were held without American athletes.

All through his presidency, the cause of peace in the Middle East was dear to Carter's heart. He told National Security Advisor Brzezinski that he would be "willing to lose the Presidency for the sake of genuine peace in the Middle East. . . ."[5]

Carter had visited the Middle East in 1973, when he was governor of Georgia. At that time, he made contacts with Arab and Israeli leaders. In 1977, he studied Middle East issues. Carter met with President Anwar Sadat of Egypt for the first time in April 1977. He met with Prime Minister Menachem Begin of Israel in July 1977.

In November 1977, Sadat made a trip to Jerusalem. Carter decided to ask both Sadat and Begin to come to the United States to talk. Both men agreed to come to Camp David in September 1978.

National Security Advisor Brzezinski said that Carter worked very hard at Camp David. He spent all his time talking to the Israelis and the Egyptians. Then, almost single-handedly, Carter wrote the peace treaty. Brzezinski called the Camp David accord "a triumph of Carter's determined mastery of enormous detail and of his perseverance."[6]

Camp David was the highlight of Carter's presidency. It was a great victory. Journalists who had been critical of Carter now praised him. "President Carter's spectacular success at Camp David not only gives his personal prestige a needed boost at a critical time, but also renews the image of the United States as a commanding world power," said a reporter.[7] Another wrote, ". . . Mr. Carter has dispelled the doubts about his ability to handle great issues."[8]

But the greatest challenge for the Carter presidency was developing in Iran, which is located in the Middle East. The United States and Iran had a long history of friendship and cooperation. Shah Mohammed Reza Pahlavi had come to power in Iran in 1940. (A shah is like a king.) His relations with the United States were good. During the 1970s, many Iranians hated the shah. They resented his farm policies, which pushed many small farmers into poverty. The shah's industrialization

Carter admires a handshake between President Sadat of Egypt (left) and Israeli Prime Minister Begin (right) at Camp David. The Camp David accords were drafted almost solely by Carter and were his greatest achievement as president.

programs benefited only a few. His Westernization of Iranian life offended religious people who saw their values crumbling. Worst of all was the SAVAK, the shah's secret police. They used torture to put down any opposition.[9]

Iranians who wanted to get rid of the shah gathered around an Islamic religious leader, the Ayatollah Ruhollah Khomeini. ("Ayatollah" is a title given to an important Islamic leader.) Khomeini had fled Iran and was living in exile in Paris, France. From there, he sent messages back to Iran. He told his followers to over-throw the government of the shah. Then, he promised, he would return to lead the country according to Islamic principles.

In November 1977, the shah of Iran visited Washington, D.C. Many Iranian students were living in the United States. Thousands of them went to Washington to express their feelings. Some liked the shah, but most hated him. The anti-shah students gath-ered around the White House. They waved signs with anti-shah slogans and shouted things like "Down with the Shah."[10]

Army helicopters circled the White House during the demonstration. Tear gas was hurled at the demonstra-tors, and tears streamed from the eyes of the invited guests, including the shah. The meeting between the shah and Carter ended with a friendly agreement. Yet from the near riot around the White House, it was clear that many Iranians passionately hated their leader.

In the months following the shah's visit, unrest spread in Iran. There were many demonstrations and riots. Carter and his advisors discussed the problem. Some of the advisors told Carter the shah would soon be overthrown and nothing could prevent it. Others pointed out that the shah had been a faithful friend of the United States for many years and a way should be found to help him. In April 1978, National Security

SOURCE DOCUMENT

Revised:
1/27/78
:30 p.m.

THE PRESIDENT'S SCHEDULE

Friday - April 28, 1978

7:30 (20 min.)	Meeting with Vice President Walter F. Mondale, Secretary Cyrus Vance, Dr. Zbigniew Brzezinski, and Mr. Hamilton Jordan - The Oval Office.
7:50	Dr. Zbigniew Brzezinski - The Oval Office.
9:00	Mr. Frank Moore - The Oval Office.
10:30	Mr. Jody Powell - The Oval Office.
11:00 (20 min.)	Mr. Charles Schultze - The Oval Office.
1:00 (30 min.)	Meeting with Editors. (Mr. Jody Powell). The Cabinet Room.
2:00 (10 min.)	Message Filming. (Mr. Barry Jagoda). The East Garden.
2:15 (15 min.)	Planting of a Cedars of Lebanon Tree. (Mr. Rex Scouten) - The Southwest Jefferson Mound.
4:30 (15 min.)	Drop-By Reception for Delegates to the 1978 Convention of the National Federation of Democratic Women. The East Room.
5:00	Depart South Grounds via Helicopter en route Camp David.

Anti- inflation
Airline Dereg
Hosp Cost Cont

Bureaucracy
Civil Service

Tax reform
Energy
SALT
S Africa
Mid East Arms
Turkey
H₂O ~~prop~~ policy

An example of President Carter's daily schedule. This one was for April 28, 1978, right around the time troubles with Iran began.

Advisor Brzezinski urged support for the shah in his struggle to stay in power.[11]

Since the shah had long been seen as a bulwark against Communism in the Middle East, every United States President since 1940 had supported him. The Iranian people knew this and began to hate the United States as much as they hated the shah.[12]

Finally, a major strike stopped everything in Iran. It seemed the entire population was in the streets, screaming their hatred of the shah and the United States. It was clear that the shah had lost control of the country. There was nothing for him to do now but run for his life, which is what he did.

In January 1979, the shah fled Iran and took refuge in the country of Morocco. Khomeini was broadcasting bitter anti-American messages from Paris. He blamed the United States for all the shah's alleged crimes. Carter ordered that any Americans who wanted to leave Iran be helped out by United States military personnel in Iran. Twenty-five thousand Americans were evacuated, but ten thousand chose to remain. Some had jobs in Iran, and some were married to Iranians. Among the Americans who remained behind were diplomats in the American embassy in Teheran, the nation's capital.

In February 1979, Khomeini returned to Teheran for a wildly triumphant victory parade. He got a hero's welcome. Meanwhile, the shah wanted to come to the United States, but Carter refused to allow it. Since hatred of the shah was so intense, there was fear that allowing him into the United States would further inflame the situation. The shah's declining health changed all this.

For six years, the shah had suffered from lymphoma, cancer of the lymph glands. His disease was controlled with drugs, but they had ceased to work. The shah's skin turned yellow as cancer attacked his liver. The shah's doctors said he could get the treatment he needed only in the United States. Carter decided to allow the shah into the United States because, as he later said, "I was told the shah was desperately ill, at the point of death."[13] Carter told the State Department to inform the Iranian government that the shah was being allowed into the United States just for medical treatment.

The Iranians who followed the new Khomeini government were enraged. They said it was all a plot to allow the shah to live in the United States and plot his return to power in Iran.

In late October 1979, the shah entered a New York hospital. The doctors said he was gravely ill and would need an operation. Angry anti-American demonstrations broke out in Teheran. Screaming crowds surged around the American embassy. Most of the demonstrators were students. At first, Iranian police kept the demonstrators from attacking the embassy. This gave Carter and his aides a false confidence.[14] The United States government expected nothing worse than a few days of noisy demonstrations, with no real threat to the embassy or its staff. Neither Carter nor most Americans really understood the Ayatollah Khomeini.

Khomeini wanted to completely take over Iran and he wanted no opposition. A good way to accomplish this was to whip up intense anti-American hatred. In his speeches, Khomeini warned his followers that the United States wanted to destroy him and his revolution. Khomeini especially hated President Carter because Carter had called the shah an "island of stability."[15]

A few hundred Iranian students came to the American embassy at 7:30 A.M. on Sunday, November 4, 1979. They began to chant, "Death to the Shah," "Death to Carter," and "Death to America."[16]

Despite troubles brewing with Iran, Carter still had time to receive Pope John Paul II at the White House.

SOURCE DOCUMENT

University of Notre Dame
Notre Dame, Indiana
Office of the President
October 10, 1979

cc Father Ted Hesburgh!

Thank you! It was one of the best days of my life.

Jimmy

Honorable Jimmy Carter
The White House
Washington, D. C.

Dear President Carter:

As one of the many who attended the White House reception for Pope John Paul II, may I say how touched all of us were by your splendid remarks, both at the prior meeting with Congress and the Judiciary and the meeting in back of the White House with the rest of us. I thought that what you had to say was superbly and eloquently said, despite the inherent difficulty of an unprecedented situation. You handled it with great sensitivity and consummate courtesy. As one Catholic who greatly enjoyed the historical moment and the splendor of the occasion, may I say again many, many thanks to you.

With continued best wishes and prayers, I am

Cordially yours,

(Rev.) Theodore M. Hesburgh, C.S.C.
President

Rev. Theodore M. Hesburgh praises Carter for his handling of Pope John Paul II's visit to the White House in 1979.

Moorhead C. Kennedy, Jr., one of the diplomats inside the American embassy, stood at a window and watched the screaming Iranians climb over the wrought iron gates. Some carried clubs and some had pistols. Huge posters of Ayatollah Khomeini bobbed among them. "I wondered to myself," Kennedy recalled, "what it would be like to die."[17]

A catastrophe was under way in Teheran.

9

THE HOSTAGE CRISIS

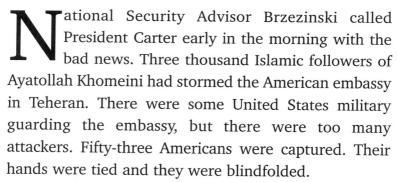

National Security Advisor Brzezinski called President Carter early in the morning with the bad news. Three thousand Islamic followers of Ayatollah Khomeini had stormed the American embassy in Teheran. There were some United States military guarding the embassy, but there were too many attackers. Fifty-three Americans were captured. Their hands were tied and they were blindfolded.

Soon there were television pictures of the incident. Blindfolded Americans were shown being shoved by angry, shouting men. The Iranians chanted "The U.S. is our enemy," and "Death to Carter." It was a sight made to "terrorize and humiliate."[1]

President Carter was beginning what he called the most difficult time of his life. From then on, he worried constantly about the safety of the hostages. "I was absolutely determined," Carter later recalled, "that I would use my utmost influence to preserve their lives."[2]

The Iranians holding the hostages demanded that the shah be sent home to be put on trial. Carter refused to do this.

The capture of the American diplomats was very shocking. If criminals inside Iran had kidnapped the Americans, it would have been different. This kidnapping was done by men who seemed to have the support of the Iranian government. The Ayatollah Khomeini was now the leader of Iran. He gave orders to a group called the Revolutionary Council. It appeared that the new government of Iran had kidnapped the Americans and was setting conditions for their release. An angry Khomeini spoke hatefully against the United States and made threats toward the hostages.

In the United States, some Iranian students marched in support of the Iranian government under Khomeini. Street fights broke out between the Iranians and angry Americans.

Carter believed that the hostages would be held for only a few days. He thought Khomeini just wanted to make a point. Then he would release the hostages. That did not happen. Khomeini seemed very pleased to be holding American hostages. Carter was told that Iran would not even talk about freeing the hostages until the shah was returned to Iran.

The shah was gravely ill in a New York hospital and

moving him anywhere would have killed him. The shah trusted the United States. The United States could not turn him over to enemies who would kill him.

The United States had military forces very close to Teheran. However, Carter feared that using these forces in a strike against Iran would result in the deaths of the hostages. From the beginning, Carter put the safety of the shah and the hostages above everything else.

SOURCE DOCUMENT

CONGRESSIONAL TELEPHONE REQUEST

TO:	Congressman Earl Hutto
DATE:	Friday, October 12, 1979
RECOMMENDED BY:	Frank Moore *Fm/pd*
PURPOSE:	Congressman Hutto would like to discuss Florida politics with you.
DATE SUBMITTED:	October 12, 1979

Looks good in N.W. Fla. - Clean sweep - Ken slate in Pensa - not a chance

— USS Lexington's replacement ~ Coral Sea - Meet some dredging - Pensacola - Ltr

— Naval Air rework facility - one of six - Contracting out - A4 fast fixed wing plane - want to keep in house.

— Sea net training - continue

— No consolidation of helicopter & other training

As leader of Carter's congressional liaison group, Frank Moore had many communications with members of Congress, such as this telephone request to Congressman Earl Hutto.

As time passed, anger grew in the United States. The Iranian flag was burned in the streets of Washington, D.C., Los Angeles, Houston, and other cities. Carter called November 5 and 6, 1979, the worst two days of his presidency.[3]

Some of Carter's political enemies began to speak out. They saw this incident as another example of the President's lack of leadership. Senator Edward "Ted" Kennedy of Massachusetts said that Carter should have known what would happen if he let the shah into the country. The Republican former governor of Texas, John Connally, said, "We can't afford to be kicked around. If appeasement were an art form, this Administration would be the Rembrandt of our time."[4]

In Iran, Khomeini mocked Carter. He said Carter did not have the "guts" to use military force to free the hostages.[5]

Carter decided to stay close to Washington during this crisis. Elections were being held in 1980, and Carter wanted to run for a second term. But he wanted to devote most of his time to trying to get the hostages out safely. Though Carter faced the challenge of Democrats like California Governor Jerry Brown and Senator Kennedy trying to get the nomination from him, he refused to campaign until the hostages were free.

Late in November 1979, Khomeini was hinting that the American hostages might be put on trial. He said they were not really diplomats. They were spies. Fear for their safety grew. If the Americans were tried as spies, they could be executed. Carter was told by his advisors in November that, as things now stood, the chances of the hostages ever getting out alive were about 50-50.[6]

In Carter's own administration, there were bitter regrets. Some were sorry that the United States had allowed the shah to come into the country for medical treatment. Aides recalled Carter himself worrying aloud that if we let the shah into the country some "group of fanatics" might "grab Americans" in Iran.[7]

A White House aide said, "We knew something like this would happen. But it's too late now. We can't move the Shah. He's got tubes hanging out of his body, they've cut him open."[8] Doctors in New York were now saying the shah needed many weeks of treatment before he could leave the country. The shah promised to leave as soon as he was able, but it would not be soon.

By Christmas 1979, the hostages had been in captivity for six weeks. Carter canceled the traditional lighting of the White House Christmas tree. He wanted to leave it dark as a symbol of sadness. Americans began tying yellow ribbons to trees, lampposts, and car radio antennas as a sign of support for the hostages. It seemed the hostage crisis was constantly on everyone's mind.

In late December, the shah left the United States to continue his medical treatment in Panama, which agreed to give him refuge. Khomeini was once again furious and sure this was a scheme to hide the shah in

Panama until the United States found a way to return him to power in Iran.

In the midst of President Carter's other concerns, a new problem was developing. Carter's younger brother, Billy, was a popular member of the First Family. Billy Carter was a good-natured farmer who used homespun humor to get a lot of publicity. People enjoyed seeing the down-to-earth brother of the President making jokes. In 1978, Billy Carter took a trip to Libya with a group of Georgia businessmen. Billy Carter was having financial problems and he accepted a job representing Libya in making sales of their oil in the United States. He was not aware that he needed to register as the agent of a foreign government to do this work.

Libya was accused by many of promoting worldwide terrorism. Some experts said that terrorists hid in Libya and made bombs later used to blow up airliners and buildings in other countries. When Billy Carter invited some of his Libyan friends to Atlanta, he was criticized for being friendly to a government that promoted terrorism. Billy Carter said that "a heap of governments support terrorists and [Libya] at least admitted it."[9]

President Carter was embarrassed by all this. He told the American people that he had no control over what his brother did.[10] A White House aide said, "[this] Billy Carter stuff is killing us."[11] This issue raged all through 1980 when Billy Carter registered as a foreign agent, someone who represented the interests of a foreign government. Finally, it was shown that he had done nothing wrong except neglect to register earlier.

Meanwhile, President Carter had cut off all oil imports from Iran, and he froze Iranian assets in American banks in November 1979. The Iranians had billions of dollars in United States banks and now they could not touch that money. These actions still did not move Iran to free the hostages. At the same time, economic problems were developing within the United States.

In the summer of 1979, inflation began to rise. Gasoline prices soared, and there were gas shortages in some areas. Since Iranian oil was no longer being sold in the United States, oil shortages developed. By April 1980, inflation rates were nearing 13 percent. With normal inflation, prices were expected to rise about 2 to 3 percent a year. That meant a loaf of bread costing seventy cents one year might cost seventy-two cents the next year. When inflation is 13 percent, that seventy-cent loaf of bread would cost seventy-nine cents the next year. When this increase is applied to all the items people buy, it becomes hard to make ends meet.

Interest rates were also very high. People who wanted to buy a house could not afford to do so. As a result, the building industry was in trouble. Automobile loans had the same high interest rates, harming the auto industry. Unemployment grew. In March 1980, over 7 million Americans were out of work. That was 7 percent of the working population. By July 1980, over 8 million

Americans were unemployed. President Carter tried to solve the growing economic crisis with voluntary price controls and other measures. The economy seemed to be spinning out of control.

In the midst of the economic crisis, the hostage situation continued in Iran. In April 1980, President Carter approved a military rescue plan to save the hostages. A small United States plane flew hundreds of miles into Iran at low altitude, then landed in the desert. The Iranians never saw it. This was a practice run for the real rescue.

The United States had detailed blueprints of all the embassy buildings in Teheran. The Central Intelligence Agency (CIA) had secret information about where every hostage was. The plan was this: Eight helicopters were to fly from United States aircraft carriers in the Gulf of Oman. The helicopters would land in a remote Iranian desert. Six C-130 transport planes would join them there. These transport planes would carry ninety members of the rescue team as well as fuel supplies. The rescue team would board the helicopters as the transport planes flew out of Iran. During the day, the helicopters would hide. The following night, trucks would meet the helicopters. Some of the rescue-team members would drive into Teheran in the trucks. The other members would remain with the helicopters. The trucks would arrive at the embassy, where the rescue would begin. The rescue team would overpower the Iranian guards and free the hostages. Then the hovering helicopters would swoop down, pick up the hostages and rescuers, and fly away. Two C-141 transport planes waited at an abandoned airstrip near Teheran to take everybody across the Iranian border to freedom.

On April 24, the eight helicopters took off on their way to the Great Iranian Salt Desert. There was trouble right away. They ran into a violent dust storm. Two helicopters stalled. The six helicopters that worked were believed to be enough to complete the mission. The rescue team could not afford to lose even one more, though.

The C-130 transports and six helicopters prepared to continue the mission. Some Iranians appeared, including a bus loaded with passengers. The Americans captured some of the Iranians, but the others got away. There was fear that the Iranians at the embassy would be warned.

Suddenly, one of the remaining helicopters refused to start. The rescue mission was called off. Five helicopters would not be enough. It was a disappointing failure. Soon it was also a tragedy. One of the remaining helicopters crashed into the nose of a C-130 transport. Both aircraft burst into flames. Eight Americans were killed. Carter later said he was haunted by memories of the disaster. He grieved especially for the loss of the brave Americans in the desert.[12]

Even though he did not want to, Carter had to begin campaigning for the Democratic nomination for President. He campaigned mainly from the White

House, while his major opponent, Senator Edward Kennedy, made speeches all over America. Kennedy demanded more government spending to help boost the economy. That was the opposite of what Carter wanted to do. He wanted to cut spending and reduce the national debt.

Kennedy won a few primary elections, but Carter won more. When Carter won renomination as the Democratic nominee, Kennedy did not give him his full support. Carter headed for the November 1980 election with a divided party. In July 1980, the Republicans

Nearing the end of his presidency, Carter waves to the delegates at the 1980 Democratic National Convention along with his wife and the Mondales.

chose former California Governor Ronald Reagan to run for President. Carter now faced the fall elections during the worst year of his presidency.

Carter said, "1980 was pure hell—the Kennedy challenge, Afghanistan, having to put the SALT Treaty on the shelf, the recession, Ronald Reagan, and the hostages . . . always the hostages! It was one crisis after another."[13]

Critics blamed the President for some of the problems. One critic concluded that Carter was "bleeding from a thousand self-inflicted wounds. He has lost the respect of Congress and made financial markets skittish."[14] Another said his record was "dreary."[15] Still another said the President was burdened with too many insupportable problems he could not overcome, including "boiling inflation, soaring interest rates, an oncoming recession, the crisis in Teheran."[16]

In September 1980, Iraq invaded Iran and bombed the Teheran airport. The Iranians accused the United States of helping Iraq make the attack. The hostage crisis only grew worse.

During the campaign debate between President Carter and Ronald Reagan, Carter felt he explained his ideas very well. Still, he believed Reagan won the debate because he reached the television audience better than Carter did.[17]

There were signs that Iran was ready to make a deal. Carter hoped the hostages would be freed before the election. Algeria spoke for the United States in direct

SOURCE DOCUMENT

THE SECRETARY OF DEFENSE
WASHINGTON, D. C. 20301

8 MAR 1977

MEMORANDUM FOR THE PRESIDENT

SUBJECT: Shortfalls in Department of Defense Outlays

Your note of March 3, 1977 requested information with respect to FY 1976 and FY 1977 shortfalls in outlays.

For FY 1976--and the transition quarter as the Federal Government moved to a new fiscal year basis--the Department of Defense fell $5.2 billion short of the projection that was made in January 1976. Of this amount $2.4 billion was attributed to the military assistance program and primarily involved foreign military sales transactions. This is a particularly difficult area to forecast, and the shortfall resulted from the fact that collections from our foreign customers exceeded our own disbursements by that amount. The remaining $2.8 billion represented an underestimate of about 2.4% relative to a total estimate of $114.2 billion for military functions. This was somewhat higher than a normal miss range of one to two percent and was probably indicative of slippages which occurred in executing contracts during that period. Such slippages were taken into consideration by the previous administration as they formulated the FY 1978 budget, and I reviewed the situation again as we developed the recent amendments.

Insofar as FY 1977 is concerned, Mike's recent statement on outlay shortfalls is based upon an October 1976 phasing plan and includes $.7 billion for DoD military functions and $2.1 billion for the military assistance program. In view of budgetary adjustments which have occurred since October, the Office of Management and Budget has recently requested that a revised monthly phasing plan be prepared. My own assessment is that this department is within approximately 1% of its plan for military functions. I have emphasized the importance of timely program execution in achieving our national security objectives and feel that we will continue to remain reasonably on target. The foreign military sales area is another matter, however, and we continue to experience difficulties in our projections. During the first four months of FY 1977, for example, collections exceeded disbursements by $2.2 billion. We have been advised by Treasury that they recognize the problems in this area and attempt to take them into consideration in developing short-term borrowing requirements. Nevertheless, we hope to develop more realistic forecasts and to improve the efficiency of our foreign military sales trust fund operation.

Harold Brown.

To Harold. I don't mind permanent non-expenditures or better collections re foreign military sales. I don't want expenditures delayed to a later F Year if we can help it. to unbalance later budgets & suffer from inflation J.C.

Secretary of Defense Harold Brown outlines shortfalls in the Defense budget. Although economic times did get tough at the end of his presidency, Carter always tried to keep the budget balanced.

negotiations for release of the hostages in exchange for freeing Iranian money frozen in American banks. However, the Iranians kept stalling in the talks.

As the November election drew closer, news programs featured many stories about the hostages. It had been one year since their capture. The American people were angry and frustrated. It appeared that only the immediate release of hostages could save the Carter presidency.

10

AFTER THE PRESIDENCY

O n election day 1980, the American hostages were still being held in Iran. Carter expected to lose the election. Early in the afternoon, exit polls were already showing a huge margin for Reagan. Jimmy Carter lost the election to Ronald Reagan in a landslide. Reagan got just under 44 million votes to Carter's roughly 36.5 million. Reagan won 489 electoral votes to Carter's 49. Independent candidate John Anderson won 7 percent of the vote. Carter captured only Georgia, Hawaii, Maryland, Minnesota, Rhode Island, West Virginia, and the District of Columbia.

Reagan was now President-elect, but Carter was still the President. During the next two months, Carter worked daily to solve the hostage crisis. Carter had agreed to exchange the hostages for $12 billion in

STATEMENT BY THE PRESIDENT

It gives me great pleasure to sign into law S. 643, the Refugee Act of 1980, which revises provisions for refugee admissions and assistance. This legislation is an important contribution to our efforts to strengthen U.S. refugee policies and programs.

The Refugee Act reflects our long tradition ~~of generosity~~ *as a haven* ~~toward~~ *for* people uprooted by persecution and political turmoil. In recent years, the number of refugees has increased greatly. Their suffering touches all and challenges us to ~~extend aid,~~ *help them,* often under difficult circumstances.

The Refugee Act improves procedures and coordination to respond to the often massive and rapidly changing refugee problems that have developed recently.

It establishes a new admissions policy that ~~eliminates current restrictions, allowing us to admit refugees of special humanitarian concern to~~ *will permit fair and equitable treatment of refugees in* the United States regardless of their country of origin. It allows us to change annual admissions levels in response to conditions overseas, policy considerations, and resources available for resettlement. The new procedures will also ensure thorough consideration of admissions questions by both the Congress and the Administration.

Moreover, the Refugee Act will help refugees in this country become self-sufficient and contributing members of society. Until now, resettlement has been done primarily by private persons and organizations. They have done an admirable job, but the large numbers of refugees arriving now create new strains and problems. Clearly, the Federal Government must ~~expand funding and coordination of~~ *play an expanded role in* refugee

One of Carter's last actions as President, the signing of the Refugee Act, provided for equal treatment of all refugees.

The Refugee Act is the result of close cooperation
between the Administration and the Congress, with important
support from those who work directly with refugees in State
and local governments and private groups. Everyone who
worked so long on its passage can be proud of this contribution
to improved international and domestic refugee programs and
to our humanitarian traditions.

Jimmy Carter

Iranian assets held in the United States. Algeria was acting as a go-between to transfer the money to Iran. On January 20, 1981, Inauguration Day, arrangements were still being made.

In Iran, three planes were sitting at the airport, waiting to take the hostages to freedom. The bank transfer was complete and the hostages were finally on their way home as Ronald Reagan took the oath of office and Jimmy Carter left the presidency.

The fifty-six-year-old former President went home to Plains, Georgia. Rosalynn Carter felt very sad that her husband had not been able to do the many things he wanted to do. "It didn't seem fair that everything we had hoped for, all our plans and dreams for the country could have been gone when the votes were counted on Election Day," she said.[1]

On their return to Plains, the Carters fixed up the house they had not lived in for many years. They sold the peanut warehouse, and Carter began work on his memoirs, *Keeping Faith: Memoirs of a President.* He also began working on the Jimmy Carter Library in Atlanta. The Carters' retirement was destined to be unusual. Unlike some former Presidents who spent their retirement years in leisure, Jimmy Carter would continue his worldwide crusade for justice and peace. Carter and his family became involved in projects to improve the living conditions of the poor. Jimmy Carter also became the adult Sunday school instructor at Maranatha Baptist Church in Sumter County, Georgia. Since 1982, more than fifty-five thousand visitors from eighty countries have heard Carter's spiritual lessons. Carter often poses challenging questions such as, "How would Christ define a successful life?" and "How do we respond to someone who is genuinely ugly and unlovable?"[2]

The Carters joined Habitat for Humanity, an organization that helps poor families become first-time home-owners. Members of Habitat, like the Carters, work alongside the family to rebuild and modernize a house in poor repair. Carter, his wife, and their daughter hammered nails and painted walls. Jimmy and Rosalynn Carter spent two summers in New York, rebuilding a burned-out city apartment. They also worked in several other cities.

Jimmy Carter supervised the fund-raising and planning for the presidential library in Atlanta. The Carter Presidential Center was dedicated on October 1, 1986. It held a collection of books, a museum, and a policy center and presented a forum for debating issues. Carter hoped that world leaders would come to discuss their problems at the center, just as Sadat and Begin had come to Camp David.

In 1987, Jimmy and Rosalynn Carter worked together on a book to help Americans deal with their retirement years. The book, *Everything to Gain: Making the Most of the Rest of Your Life,* stressed leading a useful life. Many call Jimmy Carter the best example of a retired former President. *Newsweek* described him as "the modern model of a successful ex-president of the

United States."[3] Carter has written several other books, including the most recent, *Living Faith,* his eleventh book. Published in 1996, this book urges us to "look at ourselves, our circumstances, the environment in which we live, and ask: Within my own talent and realm of possibilities, what can I find to do that would be good and lovely?"[4]

In 1988, Carter joined with former President Gerald Ford in a group called American Agenda to focus on the most important national issues and seek solutions.

Since leaving the White House, Jimmy Carter has been nominated several times for the Nobel peace prize because of his willingness to travel many miles, often to dangerous places, trying to bring peace to warring peoples. In 1987, Carter met with Soviet leader Mikhail Gorbachev to talk about Middle East problems. Carter also visited the leaders and business people of Egypt, Algeria, Israel, Syria, and Jordan.

In 1989, Carter went to Ethiopia to help settle a long and bloody civil war with rebels in Eritrea. Carter invited both sides to Atlanta to work out their differences. In the same year, he went to Panama to help make sure the elections were honest. Carter has always believed that people in every country should have the chance to honestly select their own leaders.

Carter is known all over the world as someone who can be trusted. In times of crisis he has been called, and he can often be found in a remote spot settling a dispute. In 1994, there was a crisis in Haiti. Carter had been there before to help oversee the elections that put Jean-Bertrand Aristide in office as president. Later, Aristide was overthrown by military leaders. President Bill Clinton was planning to send American military forces to return Aristide to the presidency of Haiti. But first, Jimmy Carter would lead a delegation of Americans to Haiti to try to avoid bloodshed. Carter and the others obtained promises from the generals to leave peacefully and allow the Americans to land. "I told President Clinton that we had an agreement," Carter said, "and he turned the plane around."[5] As a result, Aristide returned to power without bloodshed.

Few world tragedies have been worse than the terrible events in the African nations of Rwanda and Burundi. Bitter fighting between the Hutu and Tutsis tribes in 1994 cost the lives of half a million men, women, and children. Millions more were driven into exile as refugees. They camped in the wilderness and many died from lack of food and water. In March 1996, Jimmy Carter went to Tunisia to try to settle the nightmarish war. He met with the presidents of Burundi, Rwanda and neighboring Tanzania, Uganda, and Zaire. As a result of his intervention, many refugees were able to return home, and there has been at least the beginning of a settlement.

In 1993, Carter was asked what he thought history would say about him. "I don't know yet," he said. He did say he was proud of the Camp David agreement and normalized relations with China.[6] National Security

Advisor Brzezinski called attention to some of Carter's other solid accomplishments. Carter improved relations between the United States and Latin America with the Panama Canal treaty, which Latin America saw as fair.[7] According to Brzezinski, "the moral strength of Jimmy Carter stood out" because he always upheld the basic ideals of justice, equality, and the dignity of people.[8]

Lastly, Brzezinski gave Carter credit for saving the lives of the hostages held in Iran. Carter might have saved his presidency by taking bold military action, but some or all of the hostages might have been killed. Carter put the lives of the American hostages above his own political career.[9]

One political writer said, "In Jimmy Carter's four years as President, no American soldier died in combat. That is a great achievement—a singular one in the last fifty years."[10] Carter treasured human life. In 1996, Carter said, "For a person of faith, in particular, I believe that all decisions of war and peace must be made with the awareness that human life is never to be lightly sacrificed."[11]

When the Carter Presidential Center was opened, President Ronald Reagan said that Carter had "passion and intellect and commitment."[12] Carter truly did work tirelessly for the principles he believed in, and he continues to do so. Some people say that when Carter was President, many of his good qualities were overlooked. In the 1990s, they are finally seen and respected.

It is still too soon to decide what President Carter's

legacy will be. Yet there is a quote about him that describes him very well. When Carter gave a speech at Notre Dame University, the Reverend Theodore Hesburgh said, "[Carter is] the first president that I can remember [who has] put front and center justice and liberty for all here and around the world."[13]

Chronology

1924—Born in Plains, Georgia, on October 1.

1943—Entered United States Naval Academy at Annapolis, Maryland.

1946—Married Rosalynn Smith on July 7; Graduated from Annapolis.

1947—First child, John William Carter, born.

1950—Second son, James Earl Carter III, born.

1952—Third son, Donnel Jeffrey Carter, born; Joined crew of atomic submarine USS *Seawolf*.

1953—Resigned from United States Navy and returned to Plains.

1962—Elected to the Georgia State Senate.

1966—Ran unsuccessfully in Democratic primary for governor of Georgia.

1967—Fourth child, daughter Amy Lynn Carter, born.

1970—Elected governor of Georgia.

1976—Elected President of the United States.

1977—United States Department of Energy created.

1978—Concluded Camp David agreement, bringing peace between Israel and Egypt; Energy bills approved by Congress; SALT II Treaty written; Panama Canal treaty approved by the Senate.

1979—Diplomatic relations normalized between the United States and the People's Republic of

China; Seizure of the American embassy in Teheran, Iran, with American diplomats held hostage.

1980—Military effort to rescue hostages held in Iran fails; Lost reelection campaign for second term as President.

1981—Release of hostages held in Iran.

1986—Opening of Carter Presidential Center in Atlanta.

1987—Began worldwide missions to resolve civil wars in foreign countries.

1989—Trip to Ethiopia to mediate civil war.

1994—Trip to Haiti to restore government of democratically elected president.

1996—Trip to Tunisia to mediate Rwanda-Burundi ethnic war.

Chapter Notes

Chapter 1

1. Jimmy Carter, *Keeping Faith: Memoirs of a President* (New York: Bantam Books, 1982), p. 324.
2. Ibid., p. 283.
3. Ibid., pp. 282–284, 290.
4. Zbigniew Brzezinski, *Power and Principle: Memoirs of the National Security Advisor, 1977-1981* (New York: Farrar Straus and Giroux, 1983), p. 24.
5. Ibid., p. 263.
6. Carter, p. 391.
7. Brzezinski, p. 271.
8. Ibid.
9. Carter, p. 392.
10. Brzezinski, p. 272.
11. Ibid.
12. Carter, p. 396.
13. Ibid., p. 403.

Chapter 2

1. Hugh Carter, *Cousin Beedie and Cousin Hot: My Life with the Carter Family of Plains, Georgia* (Englewood Cliffs, N.J.: Prentice-Hall, 1978), p. 206.
2. Ibid., p. 205.
3. Ibid., p. 31.
4. Ibid.

5. Jimmy Carter, *A Government as Good as Its People* (New York: Simon & Schuster, 1977), p. 88.

6. Rosalynn Carter, *First Lady from Plains* (Boston: Houghton Mifflin, 1984), p. 22.

7. Hugh Carter, p. 7.

8. Ibid., p. 30.

9. Ibid., p. 50.

10. Ibid., p. 195.

11. Jimmy Carter, p. 75.

12. Ibid., p. 89.

13. Ibid., pp. 88–89.

Chapter 3

1. Rosalynn Carter, *First Lady from Plains* (Boston: Houghton Mifflin, 1984), p. 22.

2. Ibid.

3. Hugh Carter, *Cousin Beedie and Cousin Hot: My Life with the Carter Family of Plains, Georgia* (Englewood Cliffs, N.J.: Prentice-Hall, 1978), p. 67.

4. Ibid.

5. Rosalynn Carter, pp. 30–31.

6. Ibid.

7. Ibid.

8. Jimmy Carter, *Why Not the Best?* (Nashville: Broadman Press, 1975), p. 8.

9. Ibid., p. 10.

Chapter 4

1. Rosalynn Carter, *First Lady from Plains* (Boston: Houghton Mifflin, 1984), p. 35.

2. Jimmy Carter, *Why Not the Best?* (Nashville: Broadman Press, 1975), p. 60.

3. Rosalynn Carter, p. 36.

4. Hugh Carter, *Cousin Beedie and Cousin Hot: My Life with the Carter Family of Plains, Georgia* (Englewood Cliffs, N.J.: Prentice-Hall, 1978), p. 89.

5. Rosalynn Carter, p. 39.

6. Hugh Carter, p. 90.

7. Jimmy Carter, *Turning Point* (New York: Random House, 1992), p. 23.

8. Rosalynn Carter, p. 45.

9. Ibid., p. 49.

10. Ibid., p. 51.

11. Hugh Carter, p. 113.

12. Rosalynn Carter, p. 51.

13. Ibid., p. 52.

14. Ibid., pp. 52–53.

15. Hugh Carter, p. 117.

16. Ibid., p. 127.

17. Quoted in: Burton I. Kaufman, *The Presidency of James Earl Carter, Jr.* (Lawrence: University Press of Kansas, 1993), p. 10.

18. Ibid., p. 8.

Chapter 5

1. Hugh Carter, *Cousin Beedie and Cousin Hot: My Life with the Carter Family of Plains, Georgia* (Englewood Cliffs, N.J.: Prentice-Hall, 1978), p. 273.

2. Ibid.

3. William Lee Miller, *Yankee from Georgia* (New York: Times Books, 1978), p. 26.

4. Hugh Carter, p. 274.

5. Jimmy Carter, *Why Not the Best?* (Nashville: Broadman Press, 1975), p. 141.

6. Hugh Carter, p. 281.

7. Ibid., p. 287.

8. Ibid., p. 297.

9. Jimmy Carter, *A Government as Good as Its People* (New York: Simon & Schuster, 1977), p. 90.

10. Hugh Carter, p. 176.

11. Jimmy Carter, p. 182.

12. Ibid., p. 187.

13. Ibid., p. 255.

14. Jimmy Carter, *Keeping Faith: Memoirs of a President* (New York: Bantam Books, 1982), p. 17.

15. Ibid., p. 20.

16. Miller, p. 65.

Chapter 6

1. Hugh Carter, *Cousin Beedie and Cousin Hot: My Life with the Carter Family of Plains, Georgia* (Englewood Cliffs, N.J.: Prentice-Hall, 1978), p. 301.

2. Ibid., p. 2.

3. Jimmy Carter, *Keeping Faith: Memoirs of a President* (New York: Bantam Books, 1982), p. 77.

4. *The Wall Street Journal,* quoted in William Lee Miller, *Yankee from Georgia* (New York: Times Books, 1982), p. 26.

5. Jane Mayer and Doyle McManus, *Landslide* (Boston: Houghton Mifflin, 1988), p. 27.

6. Burton I. Kaufman, *The Presidency of James Earl Carter, Jr.* (Lawrence: University Press of Kansas, 1993), p. 34.

7. Jimmy Carter, p. 70.

8. Ibid., p. 104.

9. Statistics, 1970–1988, Blue Cross of California.

10. Jimmy Carter, p. 124.

11. John Mashek, "How Carter Spruces Up His Image," *U.S. News and World Report*, April 11, 1977, p. 43.

12. Jimmy Carter, p. 125.

13. Ibid., p. 127.

14. Hedrick Smith, "In Lance Case, the New Morality Echoes Some of the Old," *The New York Times*, September 18, 1977, p. E1.

Chapter 7

1. Jimmy Carter, *Keeping Faith: Memoirs of a President* (New York: Bantam Books, 1982), p. 143.

2. Andrei D. Sakharov, *Memoirs* (New York: Alfred A. Knopf, Inc.), 1990.

3. Quoted in Mark J. Rozell, *The Press and the Carter Presidency* (Boulder: Westview Press, 1989), p. 45.

4. Burton I. Kaufman, *The Presidency of James Earl Carter, Jr.* (Lawrence: University Press of Kansas, 1993), p. 49.

5. Zbigniew Brzezinski, *Power and Principle: Memoirs of the National Security Advisor, 1977-1981* (New York: Farrar Straus and Giroux, 1981), p. 144.

6. Hugh Carter, *Cousin Beedie and Cousin Hot: My Life with the Carter Family of Plains, Georgia* (Englewood Cliffs, N.J.: Prentice-Hall, 1978), pp. 188–189.

7. Carter, p. 159.

8. Ibid., p. 184.

Chapter 8

1. Jimmy Carter, *Keeping Faith: Memoirs of a President* (New York: Bantam Books, 1982), p. 186.

2. Ibid., p. 237.

3. Rowland Evans and Robert Novak, "The President Nobody Fears?" *Washington Post*, March 30, 1978, p. A23.

4. Marvin Stone, "Carter vs. a Dangerous World," *U.S. News and World Report*, March 5, 1979, p. 88.

5. Zbigniew Brzezinski, *Power and Principle: Memoirs of the National Security Advisor, 1977-1981* (New York: Farrar Straus and Giroux, 1981), p. 97.

6. Ibid., p. 273.

7. Hobart Rowen, "The World Looks Anew at Carter," *Washington Post*, September 21, 1978, p. A25.

8. Norman C. Miller, "The Presidential Jimmy Carter," *Wall Street Journal*, September 20, 1978, p. 22.

9. Robert D. McFadden, Joseph B. Treaster, and Maurice Carroll, *No Hiding Place: The New York Times Inside Report on the Hostage Crisis* (New York: Times Books, 1981), p. 184.

10. Hugh Carter, *Cousin Beedie and Cousin Hot: My Life with the Carter Family of Plains, Georgia* (Englewood Cliffs, N.J.: Prentice-Hall, 1978), p. 332.

11. Brzezinski, pp. 394–396.

12. McFadden et al., p. 184.

13. Ibid., p. 49.

14. Ibid., p. 177.

15. Ibid., p. 185.

16. Ibid., p. 3.

17. Ibid., p. 4.

Chapter 9

1. David Butler, Elaine Sciolino, Chris J. Harper, Fred Coleman, Eleanor Clift, Thomas M. DeFrank, and David C. Martin, "A Helpless Giant in Iran," *Newsweek*, November 19, 1979, p. 61.

2. David Briggs, "Carter's Chronicles," *The Daily Californian*, December 6–7, 1996, p. D1.

3. Butler et al., p. 61.

4. Ibid., p. 62.

5. Quoted in "No Guts?" (editorial), *Washington Post*, November 22, 1979, p. A22.

6. Butler et al., p. 61.

7. Ibid., p. 68.

8. Ibid.

9. Quoted in Burton I. Kaufman, *The Presidency of James Earl Carter, Jr.* (Lawrence: University Press of Kansas, 1993), p. 137.

10. Ibid.

11. Ibid., p. 191.

12. Jimmy Carter, *Keeping Faith: Memoirs of a President* (New York: Bantam Books, 1982), p. 518.

13. Hamilton Jordan, *Crisis: The Last Year of the Carter Presidency* (New York: G.P. Putnam's Sons, 1982), p. 1.

14. Joseph Kraft, "Self-inflicted Wounds," *Washington Post*, July 19, 1979, p. D7.

15. William Safire, "All the Help He Can Get," *New York Times*, July 12, 1979, p. A21.

16. Peter Goldman, "This Ball Game Is About Over," *Newsweek*, March 31, 1980, p. 22.

17. Carter, p. 565.

Chapter 10

1. Jimmy and Rosalynn Carter, *Everything to Gain: Making the Most of the Rest of Your Life* (New York: Random House, 1987), p. 9.

2. Cheryl Heckler-Feltz, "Bully Pulpit," *San Diego Union-Tribune*, December 6, 1996, p. E6.

3. Burton I. Kaufman, *The Presidency of James Earl Carter, Jr.* (Lawrence: University Press of Kansas, 1993), p. 213.

4. David Briggs, "Carter's Chronicles," *Daily Californian*, December 6–7, 1996, p. D1.

5. Bruce W. Nelan, "The Road to Haiti," *Time*, October 3, 1994, p. 37.

6. Kaufman, p. 210.

7. Zbigniew Brzezinski, *Power and Principle: Memoirs of the National Security Advisor, 1977-1981* (New York: Farrar Straus and Giroux, 1981), p. 144.

8. Ibid., pp. 508–509.

9. Ibid.

10. Anthony Lewis, "The King Must Die," *The New York Times*, January 11, 1981, p. E23.

11. Briggs, p. D1.

12. "Remarks at the Dedication Ceremony for the Carter Presidential Center in Atlanta, Georgia, October 1, 1986," in *Public Papers of the Presidents: Ronald Reagan, 1986* (Washington, D.C.: Office of the Federal Register, National Archives and Records Administration, 1989), 2:1310.

13. William Lee Miller, *Yankee From Georgia* (New York: Times Books, 1982), p. 162.

Further Reading

Brzezinski, Zbigniew. *Power and Principle: Memoirs of the National Security Advisor, 1977-1981.* New York: Farrar Straus and Giroux, 1981.

Carter, Hugh. *Cousin Beedie and Cousin Hot: My Life with the Carter Family of Plains, Georgia.* Englewood Cliffs, N.J.: Prentice-Hall, 1978.

Carter, Jimmy. *A Government as Good as Its People.* New York: Simon & Schuster, 1977.

———. *Keeping Faith: Memoirs of a President.* New York: Bantam Books, 1982.

———. *Living Faith.* New York: Random House, 1996.

———. *Turning Point.* New York: Random House, 1992.

———. *Why Not the Best?* Nashville, Tenn.: Broadman Press, 1975.

Carter, Rosalynn. *First Lady from Plains.* Boston: Houghton Mifflin, 1984.

Jordan, Hamilton. *Crisis: The Last Year of the Carter Presidency.* New York: G.P. Putnam's Sons, 1982.

Kaufman, Burton I. *The Presidency of James Earl Carter, Jr.* Lawrence: University Press of Kansas, 1993.

Miller, William Lee. *Yankee from Georgia.* New York: Times Books, 1982.

Rozell, Mark J. *The Press and the Carter Presidency.* Boulder, Colo.: Westview Press, 1989.

Internet Addresses

For further research on Jimmy Carter:

The Carter Center

http://www.emory.edu/CARTER_CENTER/BIOS/pcbio.htm

The Hall of Public Service

http://www.achievement.org/autodoc/page/car0bio-1

The Jimmy Carter Presidential Library

http://sunsite.unc.edu/lia/president/carter.html

White House History and Tours

http://www.whitehouse.gov/WH/glimpse/presidents/html/
jc39.html

Index

A

Aristide, Jean Bertrand, 95

B

Begin, Menachem, 5, 6, 7, 8, 67, 68
Bentsen, Lloyd, 38
Brezhnev, Leonid, 66
Brooks, Jack, 48
Brown, Jerry, 38, 79
Brzezinski, Zbigniew, 57, 71, 76, 96

C

Camp David Accord, 5-8, 67
Carter, Amy, 32, 42, 43, 54
Carter, Billy, 81
Carter, Donnel Jeffrey, 27, 54
Carter, Gloria, 12, 15
Carter, Hugh, 14, 15, 31
Carter, James Earl Sr. 9, 11, 28, 29
Carter, James Earl III, 26, 54
Carter, John William, 23, 54
Carter, Lillian, 11, 16, 54
Carter, Rosalyn, 19, 20, 22, 24, 26, 29, 30, 31, 32, 57, 58, 85, 92, 93

Carter, Ruth, 12, 15
China, 63, 65
Clinton, Bill, 95
Coleman, Julia,16
Connally, John, 79

D

Department of Energy, 50, 51

E

Eizenstadt, Stu, 40
Everything to Gain: Making the Most of the Rest of your Life, 93

F

Ford, Gerald, 39, 41, 94

G

Georgia Institute of Technology, 17
Goldwater, Barry Jr., 45
Gorbachev, Mikhail, 94
Gordy, Tom, 16

H

Habitat for Humanity, 93
Haiti, 94, 95
Hesburgh, Theodore, 74, 97

Humphrey, Hubert, 47

I
Iran crisis, 68-88

J
Jackson, Henry, 38
John Paul, Pope, 73

K
*Keeping Faith: Memoirs of a
    President*, 92
Kennedy, Edward, 79, 85
Kennedy, Moorhead Jr., 75
Khomeini, Ruhollah, 69, 71,
    75, 76, 77, 79, 80
King, Dr. Martin Luther, Jr.,
    34
Ku Klux Klan, 34

L
Lance, Bert, 52, 53, 54
Libya, 81

M
Maddox, Lester, 32
McGovern, George, 35
Mondale, Walter, 39, 85
Morehouse College, 44

N
Niebuhr, Reinhold, 34
Nixon, Richard, 37, 39

O
O'Neill, Thomas, 46

P
Pahlavi, Mohammed, 68, 69,
    70, 71, 72, 73, 77, 78, 80

Panama Canal, 59-61
Peanut Brigade, 37
Perez, Carlos Andres, 62

Q
Quitman County, 31

R
Reagan Ronald, 86, 89, 92,
    96
Rickover, Hyman, 27
Roosevelt, Theodore, 59
Rural Electrification
    Association, 9
Rwanda, 95

S
Sadat, Anwar, 5-8, 67, 68
Sakharov, Andrei, 56
Smith, Allie, 20
Smith, Edgar, 20
Southwestern Junior
    College, 17

T
Taiwan, 63, 65

U
USS *K1* 26, 27
USS *New York*, 19
USS *Pomfret*, 24, 25
USS *Seawolf*, 27

V
Vietnam War, 59

W
White Citizens Council, 30